Emotional Edge in Parenting

Your Complete Guide to Childhood Education

Surajit Sarkar

Copyright © Surajit Sarkar 2024
All Rights Reserved.

ISBN 979-8-89498-838-2

This book has been published with all efforts taken to make the material error-free after the consent of the author. However, the author and the publisher do not assume and hereby disclaim any liability to any party for any loss, damage, or disruption caused by errors or omissions, whether such errors or omissions result from negligence, accident, or any other cause.

While every effort has been made to avoid any mistake or omission, this publication is being sold on the condition and understanding that neither the author nor the publishers or printers would be liable in any manner to any person by reason of any mistake or omission in this publication or for any action taken or omitted to be taken or advice rendered or accepted on the basis of this work. For any defect in printing or binding the publishers will be liable only to replace the defective copy by another copy of this work then available.

Dedication

To Shourjya,

You are the light that brightens my every day, the smile that warms my heart, and the inspiration behind this book.

Watching you grow, learn, and flourish has been the greatest joy of my life. Your curiosity, laughter, and boundless love have taught me the true essence of parenting with the heart.

With all my love,

Surajit Sarkar

Epigraph

"To be in your children's memories tomorrow, you have to be in their lives today." — Barbara Johnson

"Children learn more from what you are than what you teach." — W.E.B. Du Bois

"The greatest gifts you can give your children are the roots of responsibility and the wings of independence." — Denis Waitley

Preface

Parenting is a journey unlike any other. It is filled with moments of joy, challenge, learning, and growth. As a parent, you strive to provide the best for your child, ensuring their happiness, well-being, and success. But what if I told you that the key to achieving all these lies in one fundamental aspect: emotion?

Welcome to "Emotional Edge in Parenting: Your Complete Guide to Childhood Education" This book is born out of decades of experience working with children, parents, and educators. Since founding the Golden Childhood Institution in 1996, I have dedicated my life to understanding the intricate dynamics of childhood education and emotional development. My journey has been enriched by the countless stories, challenges, and triumphs of the children and families I have had the privilege to work with.

This book is a comprehensive guide that delves deep into the heart of parenting and child education. It is rooted in the belief that emotional bonds form the cornerstone of a child's development. These bonds influence every aspect of a child's life, from their cognitive abilities to their social skills, and from their mental health to their academic success. By nurturing these bonds, we can unlock the true potential of our children.

In this book, you will find a blend of research-based insights, practical strategies, real-life examples, and reflective questions designed to engage and empower you as a parent or educator. Each chapter is crafted to provide a thorough understanding of key concepts while offering actionable steps to apply these insights in your daily interactions with children.

Understanding Emotional Bonds sets the foundation by exploring the significance of emotional connections and how they shape a child's world. The Role of Play in Emotional Development highlights the power of play as a medium for learning and emotional expression. Attachment Styles and Their Impact dives into the different attachment styles and their long-term effects on a child's behaviour and relationships.

Social and Emotional Learning (SEL) Strategies offers tools and techniques to teach children crucial social and emotional skills. Dealing with Common Childhood Challenges addresses the everyday hurdles parents and educators face, providing effective strategies to overcome them. Cultural Influences on Emotional Development expand our perspective by examining how different cultural practices influence a child's emotional growth.

The book also covers critical topics such as Long-Term Benefits of Secure Attachments, Addressing Emotional and Behavioural Problems, and Practical Activities to Foster Emotional Growth. Each of these chapters is designed to equip you with the knowledge and skills needed to support your child's emotional journey.

Special chapters on Understanding and Addressing Learning Disabilities and Nurturing Gifted Children provide targeted strategies for children with unique needs, ensuring that every child can thrive. Technology and Emotional Development explore the impact of digital media on children and offer guidance on maintaining a healthy balance. Building Resilience and Mindfulness and Emotional Regulation present powerful tools to help children navigate life's challenges with confidence and calm.

The collaborative effort between parents and educators is highlighted in Parent-Teacher Collaboration, emphasizing the importance of working together to support a child's development. Sibling Relationships and Emotional Development examine the dynamics between siblings and how to foster positive interactions.

Parental Self-Care underscores the necessity of self-care for effective parenting, offering practical strategies to maintain your well-being.

As you read through this book, you will find reflection questions at the end of each chapter. These questions are designed to prompt introspection and encourage you to apply the concepts to your unique context. I urge you to take the time to ponder these questions and integrate the insights into your daily life.

"Emotional Edge in Parenting" is more than just a book; it is a call to action. It invites you to embrace the power of emotional connections and to make them the cornerstone of your parenting and educational practices. By doing so, you will not only enhance your child's development but also enrich your own journey as a parent or educator.

Thank you for embarking on this journey with me. Together, let us create a nurturing environment where our children can grow, thrive, and become the best versions of themselves.

With heartfelt gratitude,

Surajit Sarkar

Prologue

When I first started working with children in 1994, I quickly realized that the traditional methods of education and parenting were missing something vital. Despite the best efforts of parents and educators, many children struggled emotionally and socially. It became clear to me that fostering emotional bonds was the missing key.

In 1996, I founded the Golden Childhood Institution in Maynaguri, West Bengal, with the mission to address this gap. Over the years, I have seen firsthand how powerful emotional connections can transform a child's life. The children I have worked with taught me invaluable lessons about resilience, empathy, and the importance of feeling understood and loved.

This prologue is an invitation to join me on a journey that delves into the heart of effective parenting and child education. "Emotional Edge in Parenting: Your Complete Guide to Childhood Education" is a culmination of over three decades of experience, research, and countless interactions with children, parents, and educators. It is a guide designed to help you navigate the complexities of raising and educating emotionally healthy and resilient children.

The foundation of this book lies in a simple yet profound belief: emotions matter. They shape our thoughts, behaviours, and interactions. For children, understanding and managing emotions is crucial for their overall development. Emotional intelligence, the ability to recognize, understand, and manage our emotions and those of others, is as important as cognitive intelligence. It is the bedrock upon which all other learning and development stand.

Through the pages of this book, you will explore the significance of emotional bonds and how they impact every aspect of a child's life. You will discover practical strategies to nurture these bonds and create an environment where children feel safe, valued, and understood. From understanding different attachment styles to implementing social and emotional learning

(SEL) strategies, each chapter offers insights and tools to support your child's emotional journey.

One of the core messages of this book is that every child is unique. Their emotional needs, strengths, and challenges vary, and our approaches to parenting and education must be flexible and adaptive. This book provides a comprehensive guide that addresses a wide range of topics, including common childhood challenges, cultural influences, learning disabilities, giftedness, technology's impact on emotional development, and more.

In "Understanding Emotional Bonds," we lay the groundwork by exploring the foundational role of emotions in child development. We delve into "The Role of Play in Emotional Development," highlighting how play is not just a leisure activity, but a critical component of learning and emotional growth. "Attachment Styles and Their Impact" provides insights into how different types of attachments shape a child's future relationships and behaviour.

"Social and Emotional Learning (SEL) Strategies" offers practical techniques for teaching children essential social and emotional skills, while "Dealing with Common Childhood Challenges" equips you with strategies to navigate everyday hurdles. "Cultural Influences on Emotional Development" broadens our understanding by examining how various cultural practices impact a child's emotional growth.

As we progress, "Long-Term Benefits of Secure Attachments" and "Addressing Emotional and Behavioural Problems" further emphasize the importance of emotional security and provide solutions for common issues. "Practical Activities to Foster Emotional Growth" and "Inculcating Values and Providing Purpose" offer actionable steps to nurture your child's emotional well-being and sense of purpose.

Special chapters on "Understanding and Addressing Learning Disabilities" and "Nurturing Gifted Children" ensure that we cater to children with unique needs, providing tailored strategies for their development. "Technology and Emotional Development" addresses the modern challenge of balancing digital engagement with emotional health. "Building Resilience" and "Mindfulness and Emotional Regulation" introduce powerful tools to help children face life's challenges with confidence and composure.

"Parent-Teacher Collaboration" underscores the importance of a unified approach to child development, emphasizing the need for strong partnerships between parents and educators. "Sibling Relationships and Emotional Development" explores the dynamics between siblings and how to foster positive interactions. Finally, "Parental Self-Care" reminds us that to be effective caregivers, we must also take care of ourselves.

As you embark on this journey through the book, you will find reflection questions at the end of each chapter. These are designed to prompt introspection and encourage you to apply the concepts to your unique context. Take the time to ponder these questions and integrate the insights into your daily life.

The journey of parenting and educating children is filled with joys, challenges, and countless moments of learning and growth. My hope is that "Emotional Edge in Parenting" will serve as a trusted companion, offering guidance, support, and inspiration as you nurture the emotional bonds that are the foundation of your child's development.

Thank you for joining me on this journey. Together, let us unlock the power of emotions to create a nurturing and supportive environment where our children can thrive and flourish.

With heartfelt gratitude,

Surajit Sarkar

Introduction

Welcome to "Emotional Edge in Parenting: Your Complete Guide to Childhood Education." In a world that is rapidly changing, the role of parents and educators in nurturing emotionally healthy and intellectually curious children has never been more crucial. This book is designed to be your comprehensive guide, equipping you with the knowledge and tools to support your child's development through the formative years.

The Power of Emotion in Childhood Education

Emotions are at the heart of our human experience, and they play a pivotal role in shaping a child's personality, behaviour, and capacity to learn. Understanding and harnessing the power of emotions can provide children with a solid foundation for a lifetime of growth, resilience, and well-being. This book explores how parents and educators can leverage emotional intelligence to create a nurturing environment that fosters both emotional and intellectual development.

Why is this Book?

"Emotional Edge in Parenting" is not just another parenting manual. It is a holistic guide that combines the latest research in child psychology, practical strategies, and real-life examples to offer a well-rounded approach to childhood education. Whether you are a parent, teacher, or caregiver, this book aims to provide you with actionable insights and effective methods to address the unique challenges and opportunities of raising and educating children today.

What You Will Learn

Throughout the chapters, we delve into various aspects of childhood education, including:

Understanding Emotional Bonds: Learn how to build strong, secure attachments with your child, which are essential for their emotional and social development.

The Role of Play in Emotional Development: Discover how playtime is not just fun but a critical part of emotional growth and learning.

Attachment Styles and Their Impact: Understand different attachment styles and their long-term effects on a child's emotional health.

Social and Emotional Learning (SEL) Strategies: Implement SEL strategies that help children manage their emotions, set goals, and establish positive relationships.

Dealing with Common Childhood Challenges: Equip yourself with practical tools to address common issues such as anxiety, aggression, defiance, and withdrawal.

Cultural Influences on Emotional Development: Explore how cultural backgrounds influence emotional expression and development, and learn to incorporate cultural sensitivity into your parenting and teaching practices.

Understanding and Addressing Learning Disabilities: Gain insights into identifying and supporting children with learning disabilities, ensuring they receive the help they need to thrive.

Nurturing Gifted Children: Learn how to support and challenge gifted children, helping them realize their full potential.

Our Approach

We believe that every child is unique, and that there is no one-size-fits-all approach to parenting and education. This book encourages you to consider your child's individual needs, strengths, and cultural background while providing you with a wide range of strategies to choose from. We aim to empower you to make informed decisions that best support your child's emotional and intellectual growth.

Join Us on This Journey

Raising and educating children is one of the most rewarding yet challenging responsibilities. By focusing on the emotional aspects of childhood education, we can help our children develop the resilience, empathy, and critical thinking skills they need to navigate the complexities of the world. Join us on this journey to discover how an emotional edge in parenting can transform your approach and make a lasting impact on your child's life.

Together, let's build a future where our children are not only academically successful but also emotionally intelligent and well-rounded individuals. Welcome to "Emotional Edge in Parenting: Your Complete Guide to Childhood Education."

Understanding emotional bonds

Contents

Chapter 1

Understanding Emotional Bonds

Introduction

Emotional bonds are the invisible threads that weave the fabric of a child's development. These bonds, formed through consistent, loving interactions, lay the foundation for a child's emotional, social, and cognitive growth. Understanding and nurturing these bonds is crucial for effective parenting and education.

This chapter explores the significance of emotional bonds, how they develop, and their profound impact on a child's life. By understanding these connections, parents and educators can create an environment where children feel secure, valued, and capable of reaching their full potential.

The Importance of Emotional Bonds

Emotional bonds are more than just feelings of affection. They are dynamic, evolving connections that influence every aspect of a child's development. These bonds provide:

1. Emotional Security: A sense of safety and trust that allows children to explore the world with confidence.

2. Social Competence: The ability to form healthy relationships and navigate social environments effectively.

3. Cognitive Development: Enhanced brain development and learning capabilities.

4. Resilience: The strength to cope with stress and adversity.

How Emotional Bonds Develop

Emotional bonds begin to form in infancy through interactions with caregivers. Key factors in their development include:

1. Consistency: Regular, predictable interactions that provide a sense of stability.

2. Responsiveness: Attentive and sensitive responses to a child's needs and signals.

3. Affection: Physical and verbal expressions of love and care.

4. Engagement: Active involvement in a child's activities and interests.

The Role of Attachment in Emotional Bonds

Attachment theory, developed by John Bowlby and Mary Ainsworth, provides a framework for understanding how emotional bonds form and influence a child's development. Attachment styles are typically categorized into four types:

1. Secure Attachment: Characterized by trust and a strong sense of security. Children with secure attachments feel confident exploring their environment, knowing they have a safe base to return to.

2. Avoidant Attachment: Marked by emotional distance and a tendency to avoid closeness. Children with avoidant attachments may appear independent but struggle with intimacy.

3. Ambivalent/Resistant Attachment: Involves anxiety and uncertainty about the caregiver's availability. Children with this attachment style often exhibit clinginess and difficulty exploring their environment.

4. Disorganized Attachment: Reflects a lack of clear attachment strategy, often due to inconsistent or traumatic caregiving. These children may show confused or contradictory behaviours.

Nurturing Secure Attachments

Creating a secure attachment involves:

1. Being Present: Spend quality time with your child, engaging in activities that interest them.

2. Showing Affection: Express love through hugs, kisses, and verbal affirmations.

3. Listening: Pay attention to your child's needs and feelings, validating their experiences.

4. Consistency: Maintain a predictable routine to provide stability and security.

5. Encouraging Exploration: Support your child's curiosity and independence while being available for support.

Impact of Emotional Bonds on Development

The strength and quality of emotional bonds affect various aspects of a child's development:

1. Emotional Regulation: Children with strong emotional bonds are better able to manage their emotions and cope with stress.

2. Social Skills: Secure attachments promote healthy social interactions and relationships.

3. Cognitive Growth: Emotional security fosters an environment conducive to learning and intellectual growth.

4. Self-Esteem: Children who feel loved and valued develop a strong sense of self-worth.

Practical Tips for Strengthening Emotional Bonds

1. Create Rituals: Establish daily or weekly traditions that reinforce family bonds, such as family dinners, bedtime stories, or weekend outings.

2. Communicate Openly: Encourage open dialogue and actively listen to your child's thoughts and feelings.

3. Play Together: Engage in play activities that your child enjoys, fostering connection and fun.

4. Support Their Interests: Show genuine interest in your child's hobbies and passions.

5. Model Positive Behaviour: Demonstrate healthy emotional regulation and social interactions.

Real-Life Example

Consider the story of Ananya, a young girl who struggled with anxiety and social interactions. Her parents, Priya and Raj, decided to focus on building a strong emotional bond with her. They spent quality time together, listening to her concerns and engaging in activities she enjoyed. Over time, Ananya became more confident and secure, excelling both academically and socially.

Reflection Questions

1. How do you currently foster emotional bonds with your child?

2. Can you recall a moment when your emotional support made a significant difference in your child's behaviour?

3. What steps can you take to strengthen your emotional connection with your child?

Conclusion

Understanding and nurturing emotional bonds is essential for fostering a child's overall development. These bonds provide the foundation for emotional security, social competence, cognitive growth, and resilience. By prioritizing these connections, parents and educators can create a nurturing environment where children thrive.

As we move forward in this book, we will explore various strategies and techniques to strengthen these bonds and support your child's emotional journey. Remember, the power of emotional bonds lies in their ability to transform lives, providing children with the confidence and security they need to succeed.

With a deeper understanding of emotional bonds, you are now equipped to create a nurturing environment that will support your child's growth and development. Let's continue this journey together, unlocking the potential within every child.

———◆◆———

John Bowlby: "Life is best organized as a series of daring ventures from a secure base."

[John Bowlby, a renowned psychiatrist and psychoanalyst, is widely recognized for his pioneering work in attachment theory. This quote underscores the importance of a secure emotional bond as the foundation from which children can confidently explore and grow.]

———◆◆———

Virginia Satir: "We need four hugs a day for survival. We need eight hugs a day for maintenance. We need twelve hugs a day for growth."

[Virginia Satir, a respected family therapist, highlights the essential role of physical and emotional connection in fostering secure attachments and promoting emotional well-being. This quote emphasizes the power of nurturing bonds in a child's development.]

———◆◆———

Chapter 2

The Role of Play in Emotional Development

Introduction

Play is often seen as a simple and enjoyable activity for children, but its significance goes far beyond mere entertainment. Play is a vital component of a child's emotional, social, and cognitive development. It provides a safe space for children to express their emotions, explore their creativity, and build essential life skills.

In this chapter, we will delve into the multifaceted role of play in emotional development. We will explore how different types of play contribute to a child's emotional well-being and offer practical tips for parents and educators to foster a play-rich environment.

The Importance of Play

Play is not just a leisure activity; it is a fundamental aspect of childhood that shapes a child's emotional landscape. Through play, children learn to:

1. Express Emotions: Play provides a safe outlet for children to express their feelings, whether they are happy, sad, angry, or scared.

2. Develop Empathy: By engaging in role-play and imaginative games, children learn to see things from others' perspectives, fostering empathy and understanding.

3. Build Social Skills: Interactive play helps children develop crucial social skills such as sharing, cooperation, and conflict resolution.

4. Enhance Creativity: Play stimulates creativity and imagination, allowing children to explore new ideas and solve problems in innovative ways.

5. Boost Resilience: Play allows children to experiment with different outcomes and learn from their mistakes, building resilience and problem-solving skills.

Types of Play and Their Emotional Benefits

1. Imaginative Play: This includes role-playing, storytelling, and pretend play. Imaginative play helps children explore different emotions and scenarios, developing their empathy and creativity.

    Example: A child pretending to be a doctor can explore feelings of care and responsibility while understanding the importance of empathy in helping others.

2. Physical Play: Activities like running, jumping, and climbing help children release energy and manage stress. Physical play also promotes the development of motor skills and body awareness.

    Example: Playing tag or participating in sports can help children experience joy, excitement, and a sense of achievement.

3. Constructive Play: Building with blocks, drawing, and crafting allow children to bring their ideas to life, fostering creativity and problem-solving skills.

    Example: Constructing a castle with blocks can give children a sense of accomplishment and encourage them to think creatively.

4. Social Play: Games that involve interaction with others, such as board games or team sports, teach children about cooperation, competition, and social norms.

Example: Playing a board game with family members can help children learn about taking turns, following rules, and handling both winning and losing gracefully.

5. Solo Play: Spending time alone with toys or books helps children develop independence and self-regulation.

   Example: A child playing alone with dolls can explore their own thoughts and feelings without external influence.

Creating a Play-Rich Environment

1. Provide a Variety of Play Materials: Offer a range of toys and resources that cater to different types of play. This could include building blocks, art supplies, sports equipment, and dress-up clothes.

   Tip: Rotate toys regularly to keep playtime interesting and stimulating.

2. Encourage Unstructured Play: Allow children time for free play without specific goals or instructions. This type of play fosters creativity and independence.

   Tip: Set aside time each day where children can choose their activities and explore their interests freely.

3. Join in the Fun: Participate in your child's play activities to strengthen your bond and model positive play behaviours.

Tip: Follow your child's lead in play and let them guide the activities. This shows that you value their ideas and creativity.

4. Create Safe Play Spaces: Ensure that play areas are safe and conducive to exploration. This includes both indoor and outdoor spaces.

   Tip: Childproof play areas and provide supervision, especially for younger children, to ensure their safety.

Practical Tips for Fostering Emotional Development Through Play

1. Observe and Reflect: Pay attention to how your child plays and the emotions they express. Use this as an opportunity to talk about their feelings and experiences.

   Tip: After a play session, ask your child how they felt during play and what they enjoyed the most.

2. Encourage Role-Play: Provide props and costumes for imaginative play, encouraging your child to explore different roles and scenarios.

   Tip: Join in role-play games and create stories together, allowing your child to take the lead.

3. Promote Cooperative Play: Organize playdates and group activities to help your child develop social skills and learn to work with others.

   Tip: Encourage games and activities that require teamwork and collaboration.

4. Support Physical Activity: Ensure your child has ample opportunities for physical play, which is crucial for managing stress and promoting overall well-being.

    Tip: Plan regular outdoor activities such as hiking, biking, or playing in the park.

5. Model Positive Play: Show your child how to engage in play positively and constructively by participating in their activities and demonstrating good sportsmanship.

    Tip: Praise your child for their efforts and creativity during play, rather than focusing solely on the outcome.

Real-Life Example

Consider the story of Rahul, a six-year-old boy who struggled with expressing his emotions. His parents, Priya and Raj, noticed that he often became frustrated and withdrawn. They decided to incorporate more imaginative play into their daily routine. They provided Rahul with costumes and props to encourage role-playing. Over time, Rahul began to express his feelings more openly through his play, creating stories and characters that reflected his emotions. His parents noticed a significant improvement in his ability to manage his feelings and interact with others.

Reflection Questions

1. What types of play does your child enjoy the most?

2. How can you incorporate more playtime into your child's daily routine?

3. In what ways can you participate in your child's play to strengthen your bond and support their emotional development?

Conclusion

Play is a powerful tool for emotional development. It allows children to explore their emotions, develop empathy, build social skills, and enhance creativity. By understanding the different types of play and their benefits, parents and educators can create a play-rich environment that supports a child's emotional growth. Remember, play is not just a pastime—it is an essential part of a child's journey towards becoming a well-rounded and emotionally healthy individual.

As we continue this journey through the book, we will explore more strategies and techniques to nurture your child's emotional development. Embrace the power of play and watch as your child thrives in a supportive and joyful environment.

Fred Rogers: "Play is often talked about as if it were a relief from serious learning. But for children, play is serious learning. Play is really the work of childhood."

[Fred Rogers, a beloved television host and educator, emphasizes the integral role of play in children's learning and emotional development. This quote highlights how play is not merely a break from learning but a fundamental part of it.]

Albert Einstein: "Play is the highest form of research."

[Albert Einstein, one of the most influential physicists, acknowledges the profound importance of play in discovery and learning. This quote underscores how play encourages exploration, creativity, and emotional growth in children.]

Chapter 3

Attachment Styles and Their Impact

Introduction

The concept of attachment is fundamental to understanding the emotional bonds that develop between children and their caregivers. These bonds, formed through consistent, responsive caregiving, play a crucial role in shaping a child's emotional, social, and cognitive development. Attachment styles, which describe the patterns of attachment behaviour exhibited by children, provide a framework for understanding how these early relationships influence a child's future.

In this chapter, we will delve into the different attachment styles, their characteristics, and their long-term impacts on a child's development. By understanding these styles, parents and educators can better support children in forming secure and healthy relationships.

The Foundations of Attachment Theory

Attachment theory, pioneered by John Bowlby and Mary Ainsworth, posits that children are biologically predisposed to form attachments with caregivers as a means of survival. These attachments serve as a secure base from which children can explore the world and a safe haven to return to when they feel threatened or distressed.

Key components of attachment theory include:

1. Proximity Maintenance: The desire to be near the people we are attached to.

2. Safe Haven: Returning to the attachment figure for comfort and safety in the face of fear or threat.

3. Secure Base: The attachment figure acts as a base of security from which the child can explore the surrounding environment.

4. Separation Distress: Anxiety that occurs in the absence of the attachment figure.

Attachment Styles

Attachment styles are classified into four main types based on the behaviour exhibited by children in response to the presence or absence of their caregiver. These styles are:

1. Secure Attachment

2. Avoidant Attachment

3. Ambivalent/Resistant Attachment

4. Disorganized Attachment

Secure Attachment

Characteristics:

Children feel confident that their caregiver will meet their needs.

They use the caregiver as a secure base for exploration.

They show distress when the caregiver leaves and are comforted upon their return.

Impact on Development:

Emotional Regulation: Securely attached children are better able to manage their emotions and cope with stress.

Social Skills: They tend to form healthier relationships with peers and adults.

Cognitive Development: Secure attachment is associated with higher levels of curiosity, problem-solving skills, and academic achievement.

Self-Esteem: These children generally have a strong sense of self-worth and confidence.

Nurturing Secure Attachment:

Consistency: Provide regular, predictable care to create a stable environment.

Responsiveness: Attend to your child's needs promptly and sensitively.

Affection: Show love and affection through physical touch, eye contact, and verbal expressions.

Engagement: Spend quality time with your child, engaging in activities they enjoy.

Avoidant Attachment

Characteristics:

Children appear emotionally distant and independent.

They show little distress when the caregiver leaves and avoid the caregiver upon return.

They may focus more on toys or activities than on people.

Impact on Development:

Emotional Regulation: Avoidantly attached children may struggle with expressing and managing emotions.

Social Skills: They may have difficulty forming close relationships and exhibit less empathy.

Cognitive Development: These children might engage less in exploratory play and exhibit lower curiosity.

Self-Esteem: They may develop a defensive self-reliance, masking feelings of insecurity.

Addressing Avoidant Attachment:

Consistency: Maintain a consistent presence in your child's life.

Encouragement: Gently encourage your child to express their feelings and seek comfort.

Patience: Be patient and understanding, allowing your child to build trust at their own pace.

Modeling: Demonstrate healthy emotional expression and relationships.

Ambivalent/Resistant Attachment

Characteristics:

Children are clingy and overly dependent on the caregiver.

They show intense distress when the caregiver leaves but are not easily comforted upon return.

They may exhibit anger or passivity towards the caregiver.

Impact on Development:

Emotional Regulation: Ambivalently attached children may experience heightened anxiety and difficulty calming themselves.

Social Skills: They might struggle with independence and show clinginess in relationships.

Cognitive Development: Their exploration and play can be hindered by their need for constant reassurance.

Self-Esteem: These children may have lower self-confidence and rely heavily on external validation.

Supporting Ambivalent Attachment:

Reassurance: Provide consistent reassurance and comfort.

Structure: Create a predictable routine to help reduce anxiety.

Encouragement: Encourage independent play and exploration in a supportive manner.

Validation: Validate your child's feelings and help them develop coping strategies.

Disorganized Attachment

Characteristics:

Children display a lack of clear attachment behaviour.

They may exhibit confused, contradictory behaviours towards the caregiver.

This style often results from inconsistent or frightening caregiving.

Impact on Development:

Emotional Regulation: Disorganized attachment is linked to difficulties in managing emotions and higher levels of distress.

Social Skills: These children may struggle with forming secure relationships and exhibit aggressive or withdrawn behaviours.

Cognitive Development: Their ability to explore and learn can be significantly impaired.

Self-Esteem: They may develop a fragmented sense of self and experience feelings of worthlessness.

Addressing Disorganized Attachment:

Safety: Ensure a safe and consistent caregiving environment.

Therapy: Seek professional support for both the child and caregiver.

Routine: Establish a stable routine to provide a sense of security.

Empathy: Show understanding and patience as the child learns to trust and regulate their emotions.

Practical Tips for Parents and Educators

1. Be Present: Spend quality time with your child, showing that you are there for them both physically and emotionally.

2. Listen Actively: Pay close attention to your child's verbal and non-verbal cues, and respond with empathy and understanding.

3. Provide Comfort: Be a source of comfort and reassurance, especially during times of stress or change.

4. Encourage Exploration: Support your child's curiosity and independence while being available for support when needed.

5. Model Healthy Relationships: Demonstrate positive relationship behaviours, such as effective communication and conflict resolution.

Real-Life Example

Consider the story of Maya, a four-year-old girl who exhibited signs of ambivalent attachment. Her parents, Sarah and David, noticed that she was extremely clingy and had difficulty separating from them. They decided to create a more structured routine and provided consistent reassurance. Over time, Maya became more confident in exploring her environment, knowing that her parents were always there for her. She gradually developed a more secure attachment style, improving her emotional regulation and social interactions.

Reflection Questions

1. Which attachment style do you think your child has developed?

2. How can you strengthen the attachment bond with your child?

3. What steps can you take to create a more secure and supportive environment for your child?

Conclusion

Understanding attachment styles and their impact is essential for fostering a child's emotional and social development. By recognizing the characteristics of different attachment styles and implementing strategies to nurture secure attachments, parents and educators can create a foundation of trust and security that supports a child's growth. As we continue this journey through the book, we will explore more strategies and techniques to nurture your child's emotional development and well-being.

Embrace the power of secure attachments and watch as your child thrives in a supportive and loving environment.

John Bowlby: "The propensity to make strong emotional bonds to particular individuals is a basic component of human nature."

[John Bowlby, the founder of attachment theory, highlights the fundamental human need to form strong emotional connections. This quote underscores the significance of attachment styles in shaping our relationships and emotional well-being.]

Brene Brown: "Connection is why we're here; it is what gives purpose and meaning to our lives."

[Brene Brown, a renowned researcher and author, emphasizes the vital role of emotional connections in providing meaning and purpose. This quote resonates with the idea that attachment styles deeply influence our ability to connect and find fulfillment in relationships.]

Chapter 4

Social and Emotional Learning (SEL) Strategies

Introduction

Social and Emotional Learning (SEL) is a crucial aspect of a child's development that goes hand in hand with academic learning. SEL equips children with the skills to manage their emotions, build healthy relationships, and make responsible decisions. By integrating SEL strategies into daily routines, parents and educators can foster a supportive environment where children thrive both emotionally and socially.

In this chapter, we will explore various SEL strategies, their benefits, and practical ways to implement them. Understanding and applying these strategies will help children develop into well-rounded individuals capable of navigating the complexities of life with resilience and empathy.

The Importance of SEL

SEL is the process through which children and adults acquire and effectively apply the knowledge, attitudes, and skills necessary to understand and manage emotions, set and achieve positive goals, feel and show empathy for others, establish and maintain positive relationships, and make responsible decisions.

The core competencies of SEL include:

1. Self-Awareness: Recognizing one's emotions, strengths, and limitations.

2. Self-Management: Regulating emotions, thoughts, and behaviours in different situations.

3. Social Awareness: Understanding and empathizing with others, including those from diverse backgrounds.

4. Relationship Skills: Establishing and maintaining healthy and rewarding relationships.

5. Responsible Decision-Making: Making ethical, constructive choices about personal and social behaviour.

Benefits of SEL

Implementing SEL strategies has numerous benefits for children:

1. Improved Academic Performance: Children who participate in SEL programs tend to perform better academically.

2. Enhanced Emotional Regulation: SEL helps children manage their emotions effectively, reducing incidents of emotional outbursts and stress.

3. Better Social Skills: Children learn to communicate, collaborate, and resolve conflicts with peers.

4. Increased Empathy: SEL fosters understanding and compassion towards others.

5. Stronger Relationships: Children develop healthy, meaningful relationships with peers and adults.

Practical SEL Strategies

1. Morning Meetings:

   Purpose: Start the day with a sense of community and belonging.

   Implementation: Begin each day with a short meeting where children can share their feelings, discuss plans for the day, and set positive intentions.

Example: "Today, I feel excited because we're going to the park. My goal is to help a friend if they need it."

2. Emotion Check-Ins:

    Purpose: Help children recognize and articulate their emotions.

    Implementation: Use tools like emotion charts or journals where children can mark or write down how they feel at different times of the day.

    Example: "I feel happy because I played a fun game at recess. I feel frustrated because I couldn't finish my homework."

3. Role-Playing Scenarios:

    Purpose: Teach empathy and problem-solving skills.

    Implementation: Create scenarios where children can act out different social situations and practice responses.

    Example: "How would you help a friend who is feeling sad? Let's role-play this situation and see different ways we can offer support."

4. Mindfulness Practices:

    Purpose: Enhance self-awareness and emotional regulation.

    Implementation: Incorporate mindfulness activities such as deep breathing, meditation, or mindful movement into the daily routine.

Example: "Let's take a few deep breaths together to calm our minds. Notice how your body feels as you breathe in and out."

5. Collaborative Projects:

Purpose: Build relationship skills and encourage teamwork.

Implementation: Assign group projects that require cooperation and collective problem-solving.

Example: "Work together to create a poster about kindness. Each person can contribute their ideas and artwork."

6. Conflict Resolution Techniques:

Purpose: Teach children how to handle disagreements constructively.

Implementation: Use techniques like "I" statements, active listening, and compromise to resolve conflicts.

Example: "Instead of saying, 'You never listen to me,' try saying, 'I feel upset when I am not heard.' Let's practice this technique together."

Implementing SEL at Home and School

1. Consistent Routines:

Establish routines that include SEL activities. Consistency helps children feel secure and understand what to expect.

Tip: Create a daily schedule that includes time for morning meetings, mindfulness, and emotion check-ins.

2. Modeling Behaviour:

    Children learn by observing adults. Model the SEL skills you want to see in your children.

    Tip: Demonstrate empathy, effective communication, and emotional regulation in your interactions with others.

3. Positive Reinforcement:

    Reinforce SEL skills by acknowledging and praising positive behaviours.

    Tip: Use specific praise, such as, "I noticed you helped your friend when they were upset. That was very kind."

4. Family and Classroom Agreements:

    Create agreements or rules that reflect SEL principles, involving children in the process.

    Tip: Have a family or classroom meeting to discuss and agree on values like respect, kindness, and responsibility.

5. Reflective Conversations:

    Encourage children to reflect on their experiences and feelings.

Tip: At the end of the day, ask questions like, "What was the best part of your day? How did you handle any challenges?"

Real-Life Example

Consider the story of Lucas, an eight-year-old boy who struggled with managing his emotions and social interactions. His teacher, Mrs. Patel, decided to integrate SEL strategies into her classroom routine. She began each day with a morning meeting, incorporated mindfulness practices, and encouraged collaborative projects. Over time, Lucas learned to articulate his feelings, empathize with his peers, and resolve conflicts constructively. His academic performance improved, and he developed stronger friendships.

Reflection Questions

1. How do you currently incorporate SEL strategies into your child's routine?

2. Which SEL strategies do you think would benefit your child the most?

3. How can you model SEL skills in your interactions with your child?

Conclusion

Social and Emotional Learning (SEL) is a vital component of a child's development. By implementing SEL strategies, parents and educators can equip children with the skills to manage their emotions, build healthy relationships, and make responsible decisions. These skills not only enhance academic performance but also contribute to overall well-being and success in life.

As we continue this journey through the book, we will explore more strategies and techniques to nurture your child's emotional development. Embrace the power of SEL and watch as your child grows into a resilient, empathetic, and well-rounded individual.

Daniel Goleman: "Emotional intelligence is the key to both personal and professional success."

[Daniel Goleman, a psychologist and author known for his work on emotional intelligence, emphasizes the crucial role of social and emotional skills in achieving success in all areas of life. This quote highlights the importance of integrating SEL strategies to foster these skills in children.]

Aristotle: "Educating the mind without educating the heart is no education at all."

[Aristotle, the ancient Greek philosopher, underscores the necessity of nurturing both intellectual and emotional capacities. This quote resonates with the theme of Social and Emotional Learning, which aims to develop well-rounded individuals by addressing both cognitive and emotional aspects of education.]

Chapter 5

Dealing with Common Childhood Challenges

Introduction

Every child faces challenges as they grow and develop. These challenges can range from everyday struggles, such as temper tantrums and sibling rivalry, to more complex issues like anxiety and bullying. How we address these challenges play a crucial role in shaping a child's emotional resilience and overall well-being.

In this chapter, we will explore common childhood challenges and provide practical strategies for parents and educators to help children navigate these difficulties. By understanding and addressing these challenges effectively, we can support children in developing the skills they need to overcome obstacles and thrive.

Understanding Childhood Challenges

Children's behaviours are influenced by a myriad of factors, including their environment, genetics, and developmental stage. Recognizing and understanding these challenges is the first step in addressing them effectively.

1. Temper Tantrums:

    Description: Intense outbursts of anger and frustration, often seen in young children.

    Causes: Temper tantrums can be triggered by a variety of factors, including tiredness, hunger, overstimulation, or the inability to communicate effectively.

2. Separation Anxiety:

    Description: Distress experienced by a child when separated from their primary caregiver.

    Causes: Separation anxiety is a normal stage of development but can be exacerbated by changes in routine, new environments, or underlying anxiety.

3. Sibling Rivalry:

   Description: Competition, jealousy, and conflict between siblings.

   Causes: Sibling rivalry can stem from competition for parental attention, differences in temperament, or developmental stages.

4. Anxiety:

   Description: Excessive worry or fear that interferes with daily activities.

   Causes: Anxiety in children can be caused by a range of factors, including genetic predisposition, environmental stressors, and traumatic experiences.

5. Bullying:

   Description: Repeated aggressive behaviour intended to harm or intimidate another child.

   Causes: Bullying can result from a desire for power, social dynamics, or a lack of empathy and social skills.

6. Defiance:

   Description: Refusal to obey rules or instructions, often accompanied by oppositional behaviour.

   Causes: Defiance can be a normal part of asserting independence but may also indicate underlying emotional or behavioural issues.

Practical Strategies for Addressing Childhood Challenges

To effectively address these challenges, it is important to implement strategies that are comprehensive, practical, and culturally sensitive.

1. Managing Temper Tantrums:

    Stay Calm: Keep your composure to help de-escalate the situation.

    Tip: Take deep breaths and speak in a calm, soothing tone.

    Acknowledge Feelings: Validate your child's emotions without giving in to demands.

    Tip: Say, "I see you're very upset. It's okay to feel angry, but we need to calm down."

    Set Clear Boundaries: Consistently enforce rules and expectations.

    Tip: Explain the rules calmly and stick to them, even during a tantrum.

    Offer Choices: Provide limited options to give your child a sense of control.

    Tip: "Do you want to put your toys away now or in five minutes?"

2. Easing Separation Anxiety:

    Practice Gradual Separation: Start with short separations and gradually increase the duration.

Tip: Leave your child with a trusted caregiver for a few minutes and gradually extend the time.

Create Goodbye Rituals: Establish a consistent and comforting routine for saying goodbye.

Tip: Develop a special handshake or hug routine.

Stay Positive: Reassure your child that you will return and express confidence in their ability to cope.

Tip: Say, "I'll be back soon, and I know you'll have fun while I'm gone."

Encourage Independence: Foster self-confidence by encouraging your child to engage in independent activities.

Tip: Praise your child for small acts of independence.

3. Reducing Sibling Rivalry:

Promote Teamwork: Encourage siblings to work together on tasks and projects.

Tip: Assign collaborative activities that require cooperation.

Celebrate Individuality: Recognize and celebrate each child's unique strengths and achievements.

Tip: Avoid comparisons and highlight each child's talents.

Set Aside One-on-One Time: Spend individual time with each child to make them feel special.

Tip: Plan regular one-on-one outings or activities.

Teach Conflict Resolution: Help siblings learn to resolve conflicts peacefully.

Tip: Model and practice active listening and compromise.

4. Addressing Anxiety:

Identify Triggers: Help your child recognize and understand what causes their anxiety.

Tip: Keep a journal of situations that trigger anxiety and discuss them.

Teach Coping Skills: Provide tools for managing anxiety, such as deep breathing and visualization.

Tip: Practice breathing exercises together and use calming imagery.

Create a Supportive Environment: Offer reassurance and avoid over-scheduling to reduce stress.

Tip: Establish a calming bedtime routine and provide a safe, quiet space for relaxation.

Seek Professional Help: If anxiety significantly impacts your child's daily life, consider consulting a mental health professional.

Tip: Look for a child therapist who specializes in anxiety.

5. Preventing and Responding to Bullying:

Promote Empathy: Teach your child to understand and respect others' feelings.

Tip: Use books and stories to discuss empathy and kindness.

Encourage Open Communication: Create a safe space for your child to talk about their experiences.

Tip: Ask open-ended questions about their day and listen without judgment.

Role-Play Scenarios: Practice how to respond to bullying situations through role-playing.

Tip: Role-play different scenarios and discuss appropriate responses.

Involve School Resources: Work with teachers and school counselors to address bullying.

Tip: Schedule meetings with school staff to develop a plan for preventing and addressing bullying.

6. Handling Defiance:

Establish Clear Expectations: Communicate rules and consequences clearly and consistently.

Tip: Use simple language and visual aids to explain rules.

Offer Choices: Give your child some control by offering acceptable options.

Tip: "Would you like to do your homework now or after dinner?"

Reinforce Positive Behaviour: Praise and reward compliance and cooperation.

Tip: Use a reward chart to track and celebrate positive behaviours.

Stay Calm and Firm: Respond to defiance with calmness and consistency.

Tip: Avoid power struggles and enforce consequences without anger.

Cultural Sensitivity in Addressing Childhood Challenges

Cultural background can significantly influence a child's behaviour and the strategies that are most effective in addressing challenges. Here are ways to incorporate cultural sensitivity:

Understand Cultural Norms:

Recognize and respect the cultural norms and values of the child's family.

Avoid imposing one's own cultural expectations and practices.

Example: Learn about the family's traditions and incorporate culturally relevant practices into interventions.

Incorporate Cultural Practices:

Use culturally relevant examples and practices in problem-solving.

Include culturally specific coping mechanisms, such as traditional relaxation techniques or familial support systems.

Example: Include cultural stories and practices in activities to make the child feel connected to their heritage.

Engage with the Community:

Involve community leaders and cultural advisors in the intervention process.

Utilize community resources, such as cultural centers and support groups, to provide additional support.

Example: Partner with local cultural organizations to create programs that support the child's emotional development.

Adapt Communication Styles:

Be mindful of different communication styles and preferences based on cultural backgrounds.

Use language that is respectful and inclusive of the child's cultural context.

Example: Use bilingual materials and involve cultural liaisons to facilitate effective communication.

Real-Life Example

Consider the case of Ali, a nine-year-old boy who struggled with anxiety and withdrawal after moving to a new country. His parents, Fatima and Ahmed, noticed his reluctance to attend school and his frequent complaints of stomachaches. They sought help from his teacher, Ms. Roberts, who worked with them to create a supportive environment.

They implemented a consistent daily routine to provide Ali with a sense of stability. Ms. Roberts introduced deep breathing exercises during class and encouraged Ali to talk about his worries. Fatima and Ahmed involved Ali in community activities that aligned with their cultural background, such as joining a local soccer team with other children from their community.

Over time, Ali's anxiety reduced, and he began to participate more actively in school and social activities. The collaborative and culturally sensitive approach helped Ali adjust to his new environment and thrive emotionally.

Reflection Questions

1. What common challenges does your child face?

2. Which strategies discussed in this chapter can help address these challenges?

3. How can you create a supportive environment to help your child overcome these challenges?

Conclusion

Dealing with common childhood challenges is an integral part of parenting and education. By understanding these challenges and implementing effective strategies, parents and educators can support children in developing the skills they need to overcome obstacles and thrive. Remember, each child is unique, and it is essential to adapt these strategies to fit their individual needs.

As we continue this journey through the book, we will explore more techniques and approaches to nurture your child's emotional development and well-being. Embrace the process of addressing challenges with patience and empathy, and watch your child grow into a resilient and confident individual.

Haim Ginott: "Children are like wet cement. Whatever falls on them makes an impression."

[Haim Ginott, a renowned psychologist and educator, emphasizes the lasting impact that experiences and interactions have on children. This quote highlights the importance of how we address and manage common childhood challenges to ensure positive development.]

Fred Rogers: "Anything that's human is mentionable, and anything that is mentionable can be more manageable. When we can talk about our feelings, they become less overwhelming, less upsetting, and less scary."

[Fred Rogers, beloved television host and advocate for children's emotional well-being, underscores the value of open communication about feelings and challenges. This quote aligns with the theme of addressing childhood challenges through understanding and empathy.]

Chapter 6

Cultural Influences on Emotional Development

Introduction

Culture plays a significant role in shaping a child's emotional development. From family traditions and social norms to language and community values, cultural influences permeate every aspect of a child's life. Understanding these influences helps parents and educators create supportive environments that respect and nurture a child's cultural identity while promoting emotional well-being.

In this chapter, we will explore how different cultural practices and beliefs impact emotional development. We will examine various cultural influences, provide practical strategies for fostering emotional growth in diverse cultural contexts, and highlight the importance of cultural sensitivity in parenting and education.

The Role of Culture in Emotional Development

Culture encompasses the beliefs, values, practices, and social behaviours of a particular group or society. It shapes how emotions are expressed, understood, and managed. Key aspects of culture that influence emotional development include:

1. Family Dynamics: The structure and roles within a family, including expectations, communication styles, and disciplinary practices.

2. Social Norms: Accepted behaviours and attitudes within a community or society.

3. Language: The words and expressions used to describe emotions and experiences.

4. Rituals and Traditions: Ceremonies, celebrations, and routines that reinforce cultural values and emotional connections.

5. Community Values: Collective beliefs about what is important and valued in a society.

Cultural Differences in Emotional Expression

Different cultures have distinct ways of expressing and interpreting emotions. Understanding these differences is crucial for fostering emotional development in children from diverse backgrounds. Here are some examples:

1. Individualistic Cultures:

    Emphasis on personal achievements, independence, and self-expression.

    Example: In the United States, children are often encouraged to express their emotions openly and assert their individuality.

2. Collectivist Cultures:

    Emphasis on group harmony, interdependence, and respect for authority.

    Example: In Japan, children may be taught to prioritize group harmony and avoid expressing emotions that could disrupt social cohesion.

3. High-Context Cultures:

    Reliance on non-verbal cues and context to convey meaning.

    Example: In many Middle Eastern cultures, emotions are often communicated through body language and tone rather than explicit words.

4. Low-Context Cultures:

   Emphasis on direct and explicit communication.

   Example: In Germany, clear and direct expression of emotions and thoughts are valued.

Practical Strategies for Fostering Emotional Development in Diverse Cultural Contexts

1. Cultural Awareness and Sensitivity:

   Understand and respect the cultural background of the child and family.

   Tip: Learn about the cultural practices, values, and beliefs that influence the child's upbringing.

2. Inclusive Communication:

   Use culturally appropriate language and expressions to discuss emotions.

   Tip: Incorporate the child's native language and culturally relevant metaphors when talking about feelings.

3. Celebrating Cultural Traditions:

   Integrate cultural rituals and traditions into daily routines to reinforce cultural identity and emotional bonds.

   Tip: Celebrate cultural holidays, participate in traditional activities, and share stories from the child's cultural heritage.

4. Modeling Respectful Behaviour:

    Demonstrate respect for cultural diversity through your actions and words.

    Tip: Show interest in learning about different cultures and encourage children to do the same.

5. Encouraging Cultural Pride:

    Foster a sense of pride in the child's cultural heritage.

    Tip: Highlight the strengths and positive aspects of the child's culture and provide opportunities for them to share their cultural background with others.

6. Creating a Supportive Environment:

    Build a nurturing environment that respects and values cultural differences.

    Tip: Ensure that cultural diversity is represented in books, toys, and classroom materials.

7. Collaborating with Families and Communities:

    Work closely with families and community members to support the child's emotional development.

    Tip: Involve parents and community leaders in planning activities that reflect cultural values and practices.

Real-Life Examples

1. Indian Family Rituals:

    Example: In Indian culture, family rituals such as evening prayers, festivals like Diwali, and storytelling traditions help reinforce family bonds and provide a sense of security and continuity for children.

2. African Community Values:

    Example: In many African cultures, the concept of "Ubuntu" emphasizes communal relationships and mutual support. Children are taught the importance of empathy, cooperation, and caring for others from a young age.

3. Latino Cultural Celebrations:

    Example: In Latino cultures, celebrations like Quinceañeras and Día de los Muertos involve extended family and community, providing children with a strong sense of cultural identity and belonging.

4. Chinese Respect for Elders:

    Example: In Chinese culture, respecting elders is a core value. Children learn to show respect and deference to older family members, which helps them understand and manage their emotions in hierarchical relationships.

Consider the case of Maya, a seven-year-old girl from a South Asian family who struggled with an emotional expression at school. Her parents, Priya and Raj, adhered to cultural norms that valued emotional restraint and respect for authority. Maya's teacher, Ms. Johnson, noticed that Maya was hesitant to express her feelings and often seemed withdrawn.

Ms. Johnson engaged in conversations with Priya and Raj to understand their cultural background and parenting practices. She incorporated aspects of Maya's cultural heritage into the classroom by including stories and activities from South Asian cultures. Ms. Johnson also respected the family's values while encouraging Maya to express her emotions through culturally appropriate methods, such as storytelling and drawing.

Priya and Raj attended cultural competence workshops organized by the school, which helped them understand the importance of emotional expression in their child's development. They began to balance their cultural practices with strategies that supported Maya's emotional growth.

Over time, Maya became more comfortable expressing her feelings, and her emotional well-being improved significantly. The culturally sensitive approach taken by Ms. Johnson and Maya's parents played a crucial role in supporting her emotional development.

Reflection Questions

1. How does your cultural background influence your parenting or teaching style?

2. What cultural traditions or practices are important to your family or community?

3. How can you incorporate these traditions into your child's daily routine to support their emotional development?

Conclusion

Culture plays a pivotal role in shaping a child's emotional development. By understanding and respecting cultural influences, parents and educators can create supportive environments that nurture a child's emotional well-being and cultural identity. Embracing cultural diversity and incorporating culturally relevant practices into daily routines can strengthen emotional bonds and promote a sense of belonging.

As we continue this journey through the book, we will explore more strategies and techniques to support your child's emotional development. Embrace the richness of cultural diversity and watch as your child grows into a resilient, empathetic, and culturally aware individual.

———◆◆———

Carl Jung: "Even a happy life cannot be without a measure of darkness, and the word 'happy' would lose its meaning if it were not balanced by sadness. It is far better to take things as they come along with patience and equanimity."

[Carl Jung, a pioneering psychologist, speaks to the balance of emotions shaped by cultural contexts. This quote resonates with the understanding that cultural influences play a critical role in shaping how children perceive and manage their emotions.]

Maya Angelou: "We all should know that diversity makes for a rich tapestry, and we must understand that all the threads of the tapestry are equal in value no matter their color."

[Maya Angelou, celebrated poet and civil rights activist, emphasizes the importance of diversity and equality. This quote highlights how cultural influences contribute to the richness of emotional development and the need to value every cultural thread in a child's upbringing.]

Chapter 7

Long-Term Benefits of Secure Attachments

Introduction

The bonds we form in early childhood lay the foundation for our emotional, social, and cognitive development. Secure attachments, characterized by a strong, trusting relationship with caregivers, are crucial for a child's overall well-being. These early bonds have long-term benefits that extend into adolescence and adulthood, shaping our ability to form healthy relationships, manage emotions, and navigate life's challenges.

In this chapter, we will explore the long-term benefits of secure attachments. We will discuss how these attachments influence various aspects of a child's development and provide practical strategies for fostering secure attachments. By understanding the importance of secure attachments, parents and educators can create nurturing environments that support a child's growth and success.

The Importance of Secure Attachments

Secure attachments provide a child with a sense of safety and trust, which are essential for healthy development. These attachments are formed through consistent, responsive caregiving and are characterized by the following key elements:

1. Trust: The child trusts that their caregiver will meet their needs and provide comfort and support.

2. Safety: The child feels safe to explore their environment, knowing they can return to their caregiver for reassurance.

3. Emotional Availability: The caregiver is emotionally available and responsive to the child's needs and signals.

4. Consistent Care: The caregiver provides consistent, predictable care, creating a stable environment for the child.

Long-Term Benefits of Secure Attachments

1. Emotional Regulation:

    Secure attachments help children develop the ability to regulate their emotions effectively. They learn to manage stress, cope with challenges, and recover from setbacks. As they grow, these children tend to exhibit lower levels of anxiety and depression.

    Example: Sarah, who had a secure attachment with her parents, developed strong emotional regulation skills. As a teenager, she was able to handle academic pressures and social challenges with resilience and confidence.

2. Social Competence:

    Children with secure attachments are more likely to develop positive social skills. They form healthy relationships with peers and adults, show empathy and cooperation, and navigate social situations effectively.

    Example: Alex, who experienced a secure attachment with his caregivers, was well-liked by his peers and teachers. He exhibited empathy, resolved conflicts peacefully, and maintained strong friendships.

3. Cognitive Development:

    Secure attachments provide a foundation for cognitive growth. Children feel safe to explore and learn, leading to enhanced curiosity, problem-solving abilities, and academic achievement.

    Example: Mia, who had a secure attachment with her parents, demonstrated a strong love for learning. She excelled academically and was eager to explore new subjects and activities.

4. Self-Esteem:

    A secure attachment fosters a positive self-image and high self-esteem. Children feel valued and confident in their abilities, which influences their overall sense of self-worth.

    Example: Daniel, who grew up with a secure attachment to his caregivers, had high self-esteem. He believed in his capabilities and pursued his goals with determination and optimism.

5. Resilience:

    Securely attached children are better equipped to handle adversity. They develop resilience, allowing them to bounce back from difficulties and adapt to changing circumstances.

    Example: Emily, who had a secure attachment with her parents, demonstrated remarkable resilience. She navigated family moves, changes in schools, and personal losses with strength and adaptability.

Practical Strategies for Fostering Secure Attachments

1. Be Consistent:

    Provide consistent care and establish predictable routines to create a stable environment.

    Tip: Maintain regular meal times, bedtime routines, and daily activities to help your child feel secure.

2. Respond to Needs:

    Be attentive and responsive to your child's needs and signals. Offer comfort and support when they are distressed.

    Tip: If your child is upset, acknowledge their feelings and provide reassurance. For example, "I see you're scared. I'm here with you, and you're safe."

3. Show Affection:

    Express love and affection through physical touch, eye contact, and verbal affirmations.

    Tip: Give hugs, hold hands, and use phrases like "I love you" and "I'm proud of you" regularly.

4. Encourage Exploration:

    Support your child's curiosity and independence while being available for reassurance and guidance.

    Tip: Provide a safe environment for exploration and be there to celebrate their discoveries and achievements.

5. Create Quality Time:

    Spend dedicated time with your child, engaging in activities they enjoy and building a strong emotional connection.

    Tip: Plan regular one-on-one time, such as reading together, playing games, or going for walks.

6. Model Positive Behaviour:

    Demonstrate healthy emotional regulation and social interactions through your own behaviour.

    Tip: Show how to handle emotions calmly and communicate respectfully with others.

Real-Life Example

Consider the story of Leah, a five-year-old girl who had a secure attachment with her mother, Maria. Maria consistently responded to Leah's needs, providing comfort and support during times of distress. She also encouraged Leah's curiosity by exploring new activities together and celebrating her achievements. As Leah grew, she developed strong emotional regulation skills, social competence, and resilience. She navigated the transition to school with confidence, made friends easily, and excelled academically. The secure attachment with her mother provided Leah with a strong foundation for her continued growth and success.

Reflection Questions

1. What steps can you take to strengthen your emotional connection with your child?

2. How can you create a consistent and supportive environment for your child?

3. What strategies can you implement to encourage your child's exploration and independence?

Conclusion

Secure attachments are fundamental to a child's long-term emotional, social, and cognitive development. By fostering these attachments through consistent, responsive caregiving, parents and educators can create a foundation of trust and security that supports a child's growth and success. The long-term benefits of secure attachments include improved emotional regulation, social competence, cognitive development, self-esteem, and resilience.

As we continue this journey through the book, we will explore more strategies and techniques to nurture your child's emotional development. Embrace the importance of secure attachments, and watch as your child thrives in a supportive and loving environment.

John Bowlby: "Intimate attachments to other human beings are the hub around which a person's life revolves, not only when he is an infant or toddler or schoolchild but throughout his adolescence and his years of maturity as well, and on into old age."

[John Bowlby, the founder of attachment theory, underscores the lifelong impact of secure attachments. This quote highlights how early emotional bonds shape an individual's relationships and emotional well-being throughout their life.]

Jane Goodall: "What you do makes a difference, and you have to decide what kind of difference you want to make."

[Jane Goodall, renowned primatologist and anthropologist, speaks to the long-term impact of our actions and relationships. This quote resonates with the theme that secure attachments formed in early childhood have lasting benefits on an individual's life, influencing their ability to form healthy relationships and contribute positively to society.]

Chapter 8

Addressing Emotional and Behavioural Problems

Introduction

Emotional and behavioural problems are common among children and can manifest in various ways, such as anxiety, aggression, defiance, and withdrawal. These issues can significantly impact a child's development and well-being if not addressed effectively. Understanding the root causes and implementing appropriate strategies can help parents and educators support children in overcoming these challenges.

In this chapter, we will explore common emotional and behavioural problems in children, their underlying causes, and practical strategies for addressing them. By creating a supportive and responsive environment, we can help children develop the skills they need to manage their emotions and behaviours effectively.

Understanding Emotional and Behavioural Problems

Emotional and behavioural problems in children can stem from multiple factors, including genetic predispositions, environmental influences, and developmental stages. Early identification and intervention are key to helping children navigate these challenges.

1. Anxiety:

    Description: Excessive worry or fear that interferes with daily activities.

    Symptoms: Restlessness, irritability, difficulty concentrating, physical complaints (e.g., stomachaches, headaches).

2. Aggression:

    Description: Hostile or violent behaviour towards others.

Symptoms: Hitting, biting, shouting, temper tantrums.

3. Defiance:

   Description: Refusal to obey rules or instructions, often accompanied by oppositional behaviour.

   Symptoms: Arguing, refusing to follow directions, deliberate disobedience.

4. Withdrawal:

   Description: Avoidance of social interactions and activities.

   Symptoms: Isolating oneself, lack of interest in activities, difficulty making friends.

5. Attention-Deficit/Hyperactivity Disorder (ADHD):

   Description: A neurodevelopmental disorder characterized by inattention, hyperactivity, and impulsivity.

   Symptoms: Difficulty staying focused, excessive movement, impulsive actions.

6. Oppositional Defiant Disorder (ODD):

   Symptoms: Frequent temper tantrums, argumentative behaviour, refusal to comply with rules, and deliberate attempts to annoy others.

   Understanding: ODD can be a response to inconsistent discipline, lack of structure, or underlying emotional issues.

7. Conduct Disorder:

    Symptoms: Aggressive behaviour, deceitfulness, theft, and serious violations of rules.

    Understanding: This disorder often requires comprehensive intervention strategies due to its complexity and severity.

Understanding the Root Causes

Emotional and behavioural problems can arise from various factors, including:

1. Biological Factors:

    Genetic predisposition, brain chemistry, and neurodevelopmental disorders can contribute to emotional and behavioural issues.

2. Environmental Factors:

    Family dynamics, parenting styles, and exposure to stress or trauma can influence a child's emotional and behavioural responses.

3. Psychological Factors:

    A child's temperament, coping skills, and past experiences play a role in how they manage emotions and behaviours.

Practical Strategies for Addressing Emotional and Behavioural Problems

To effectively address these issues, it is essential to implement strategies that are detailed, practical, and culturally sensitive.

1. Anxiety:

    Identify Triggers:

    Help your child recognize what causes their anxiety.

    Tip: Keep a journal of situations that trigger anxiety and discuss them.

    Teach Coping Skills:

    Provide tools for managing anxiety, such as deep breathing and visualization.

    Tip: Practice breathing exercises together and use calming imagery.

    Create a Supportive Environment:

    Offer reassurance and avoid over-scheduling to reduce stress.

    Tip: Establish a calming bedtime routine and provide a safe, quiet space for relaxation.

    Seek Professional Help:

    If anxiety significantly impacts your child's daily life, consider consulting a mental health professional.

    Tip: Look for a child therapist who specializes in anxiety.

2. Aggression:

    Set Clear Boundaries:

    Communicate rules and consequences clearly and consistently.

Tip: Use simple language and visual aids to explain rules.

Model Calm Behaviour:

Demonstrate how to handle anger and frustration constructively.

Tip: Show calm responses to stressful situations and discuss how to manage anger.

Teach Alternative Behaviours:

Help your child learn appropriate ways to express their feelings.

Tip: Use role-playing to practice expressing emotions without aggression.

Reinforce Positive Behaviour:

Praise and reward positive interactions and non-aggressive behaviours.

Tip: Use a reward chart to track and celebrate positive behaviours.

3. Defiance:

Establish Clear Expectations:

Communicate rules and consequences clearly and consistently.

Tip: Use simple language and visual aids to explain rules.

Offer Choices:

Give your child some control by offering acceptable options.

Tip: "Would you like to do your homework now or after dinner?"

Reinforce Positive Behaviour:

Praise and reward compliance and cooperation.

Tip: Use a reward chart to track and celebrate positive behaviours.

Stay Calm and Firm:

Respond to defiance with calmness and consistency.

Tip: Avoid power struggles and enforce consequences without anger.

4. Withdrawal:

Encourage Social Interaction:

Provide opportunities for your child to engage in social activities.

Tip: Arrange playdates, join clubs, or participate in group activities.

Validate Feelings:

Acknowledge your child's feelings and encourage open communication.

Tip: Say, "I understand you feel shy. Let's think of ways to make you feel more comfortable."

Gradual Exposure:

Gradually introduce your child to new social situations to build their confidence.

Tip: Start with small, manageable social interactions and increase gradually.

Seek Professional Help:

If withdrawal significantly impacts your child's daily life, consider consulting a mental health professional.

Tip: Look for a child therapist who specializes in social anxiety.

5. ADHD:

Structure and Routine:

Establish a consistent daily schedule to provide stability and predictability.

Tip: Use visual schedules and timers to help your child stay on track.

Break Tasks into Manageable Steps:

Simplify tasks by breaking them down into smaller, more manageable steps.

Tip: Provide clear, step-by-step instructions and offer frequent breaks.

Positive Reinforcement:

Praise and reward positive behaviours and accomplishments.

Tip: Use a reward system to motivate and reinforce desired behaviours.

Collaborate with Educators:

Work closely with teachers to implement strategies that support your child's learning.

Tip: Develop an individualized education plan (IEP) or 504 plan if needed.

6. Oppositional Defiant Disorder (ODD):

Establish Clear Boundaries:

Set clear and consistent rules regarding acceptable behaviour.

Use logical consequences to reinforce these boundaries.

Example: Create a behaviour contract with the child that outlines expected behaviours and consequences.

Foster Positive Relationships:

Build strong, positive relationships through quality time and open communication.

Encourage cooperative activities that require teamwork and collaboration.

Example: Engage in family activities that promote bonding, such as game nights or outdoor adventures.

Teach Conflict Resolution Skills:

Guide children in resolving conflicts through negotiation and problem-solving.

Use role-playing to practice these skills in a safe environment.

Example: Role-play different scenarios where the child practices resolving conflicts calmly and respectfully.

7. Conduct Disorder:

Seek Comprehensive Intervention:

Engage in multi-faceted interventions involving mental health professionals, educators, and family members.

Develop a comprehensive treatment plan that includes therapy, medication (if necessary), and consistent discipline.

Example: Collaborate with a multidisciplinary team to create a personalized intervention plan.

Address Underlying Issues:

Explore potential underlying issues such as trauma, abuse, or family conflict.

Use therapeutic approaches like cognitive-behavioural therapy (CBT) to address these issues.

Example: Work with a trauma-informed therapist to address past experiences that may contribute to the child's behaviour.

Promote Social Skills:

Encourage participation in structured group activities to build social skills.

Provide opportunities for positive peer interactions and mentorship.

Example: Enroll the child in social skills groups or mentoring programs to develop positive relationships.

Cultural Sensitivity in Addressing Emotional and Behavioural Problems

Cultural context significantly influences how emotional and behavioural problems manifest and are perceived. Incorporating cultural sensitivity is crucial in effectively addressing these issues.

Understand Cultural Norms:

Recognize and respect the cultural values and norms of the child's family.

Avoid imposing one's own cultural expectations and practices.

Example: Learn about the family's cultural background and incorporate culturally relevant practices into interventions.

Incorporate Cultural Practices:

Use culturally relevant examples and practices in interventions.

Include traditional coping mechanisms and support systems, such as community elders or spiritual leaders.

Example: Integrate cultural rituals and practices into therapy sessions to make the child feel more comfortable.

Engage with the Community:

Involve community leaders and cultural advisors in the intervention process.

Utilize community resources such as cultural centers and support groups to provide additional support.

Example: Partner with local cultural organizations to create programs that support the child's emotional development.

Adapt Communication Styles:

Be mindful of different communication styles and preferences based on cultural backgrounds.

Use language that is respectful and inclusive of the child's cultural context.

Example: Use bilingual materials and involve cultural liaisons to facilitate effective communication.

Real-Life Example

Consider the case of Priya, a twelve-year-old girl experiencing symptoms of depression and anxiety after her family relocated to a new country. Her parents, Raj and Meera, noticed her withdrawal from social activities and frequent complaints of feeling unwell. They sought help from her school counselor, Mr. Thompson, who worked with them to create a supportive and culturally sensitive environment.

Mr. Thompson introduced mindfulness exercises in Priya's routine and encouraged her to keep a feelings journal. Raj and Meera involved Priya in community events with other families from their cultural background, helping her feel more connected and supported. They also attended family therapy sessions to address the stress of the move and develop coping strategies.

Over time, Priya's symptoms improved, and she became more engaged in school and social activities. The collaborative and culturally sensitive approach helped Priya adjust to her new environment and thrive emotionally.

Reflection Questions

1. What emotional or behavioural problems has your child faced?

2. Which strategies discussed in this chapter can you apply to help your child?

3. How can you create a supportive environment to address your child's emotional and behavioural challenges?

Conclusion

Addressing emotional and behavioural problems is a crucial aspect of parenting and education. By understanding the underlying causes and implementing effective strategies, parents and educators can support children in developing the skills they need to manage their emotions and behaviours. Remember, each child is unique, and it is essential to adapt these strategies to fit their individual needs.

As we continue this journey through the book, we will explore more techniques and approaches to nurture your child's emotional development and well-being. Embrace the process of addressing challenges with patience and empathy, and watch your child grow into a resilient and confident individual.

———◆◆———

Carl Rogers: "The curious paradox is that when I accept myself just as I am, then I can change."

[Carl Rogers, a pioneering psychologist in the field of humanistic psychology, emphasizes the importance of acceptance in the process of change. This quote aligns with the theme of addressing emotional and behavioural problems by fostering self-acceptance and understanding as a foundation for growth and improvement.]

Nelson Mandela: "Courage is not the absence of fear, but the triumph over it. The brave man is not he who does not feel afraid, but he who conquers that fear."

[Nelson Mandela, the revered leader and advocate for peace and justice, highlights the importance of courage and resilience in facing challenges. This quote resonates with the theme of addressing emotional and behavioural problems by encouraging children to confront and overcome their fears with support and determination.]

Chapter 9

Practical Activities to Foster Emotional Growth

Introduction

Children learn and grow through experiences that shape their emotional, social, and cognitive development. Engaging in practical activities that promote emotional growth is essential for helping children understand and manage their emotions, build healthy relationships, and develop resilience. This chapter provides a variety of activities designed to foster emotional growth, offering parents and educators valuable tools to support children's emotional well-being.

In this chapter, we will explore a range of practical activities tailored to different age groups and developmental stages. These activities are designed to be fun and engaging while promoting emotional awareness, empathy, social skills, and emotional regulation.

Activities for Emotional Awareness

1. Emotion Wheel:

   Purpose: Help children identify and articulate their emotions.

   Materials: Printable emotion wheel, markers.

   Instructions: Create an emotion wheel with different sections representing various emotions (e.g., happy, sad, angry, scared). Ask your child to color in the section that represents how they are feeling and discuss why they chose that emotion.

   Tip: Use this activity regularly to help your child become more aware of their emotions.

2. Feelings Journal:

   Purpose: Encourage children to express their emotions through writing or drawing.

   Materials: Notebook, pens, crayons.

Instructions: Provide your child with a journal and encourage them to write or draw about their feelings each day. Discuss their entries with them, offering support and validation.

Tip: Create a routine where you and your child share your journal entries together.

3. Emotion Charades:

Purpose: Teach children to recognize and express emotions through body language.

Materials: Emotion cards (printed or homemade).

Instructions: Write different emotions on cards (e.g., happy, sad, excited, frustrated). Take turns drawing a card and acting out the emotion without using words while the other person guesses the emotion.

Tip: Discuss how body language and facial expressions convey emotions.

Activities for Empathy

1. Storytelling with Empathy:

Purpose: Teach children to understand and empathize with others' feelings.

Materials: Storybooks, puppets, or toys.

Instructions: Read stories that highlight different emotions and discuss the characters' feelings. Use puppets or toys to reenact the stories, emphasizing empathy and understanding.

Tip: Ask questions like, "How do you think this character feels? Why?"

2. Acts of Kindness:

Purpose: Encourage empathy and kindness towards others.

Materials: Paper, markers, kindness jar.

Instructions: Create a kindness jar where your child can add a note each time they do something kind to someone else. Celebrate these acts of kindness regularly.

Tip: Lead by example and participate in acts of kindness together.

3. Empathy Map:

Purpose: Help children understand different perspectives.

Materials: Large paper, markers.

Instructions: Draw a map with a person in the center and sections around it labeled "What they see," "What they feel," "What they think," and "What they need." Discuss a specific situation and fill out the map together.

Tip: Use real-life scenarios or stories to make the activity more relatable.

Activities for Social Skills

1. Cooperative Games:

    Purpose: Promote teamwork and communication.

    Materials: Board games, building blocks, sports equipment.

    Instructions: Engage in games that require cooperation, such as building a structure together or playing team sports. Emphasize the importance of working together and communicating effectively.

    Tip: Praise teamwork and discuss ways to improve collaboration.

2. Role-Playing:

    Purpose: Teach children how to navigate social situations and resolve conflicts.

    Materials: Costumes, props.

    Instructions: Role-play common social scenarios, such as making new friends, sharing toys, or resolving disagreements. Encourage your child to practice different responses and discuss the outcomes.

    Tip: Use this activity to address specific social challenges your child may face.

3. Friendship Bracelets:

    Purpose: Foster friendship and social connection.

    Materials: String, beads.

Instructions: Make friendship bracelets together and discuss the qualities of a good friend. Encourage your child to give the bracelets to their friends as a gesture of appreciation.

Tip: Use this activity to talk about the importance of kindness and support in friendships.

Activities for Emotional Regulation

1. Mindful Breathing:

    Purpose: Teach children to manage stress and regulate their emotions.

    Materials: Quiet space, comfortable seating.

    Instructions: Practice deep breathing exercises together. Inhale deeply through the nose, hold for a few seconds, and exhale slowly through the mouth. Encourage your child to focus on their breath and how it feels.

    Tip: Use this technique during moments of stress or before bedtime to promote relaxation.

2. Calm Down Kit:

    Purpose: Provide tools for children to use when they feel overwhelmed.

    Materials: Small box or bag, sensory toys, stress balls, coloring books, fidget tools.

Instructions: Create a calm down kit with items that help your child relax and self-soothe. Encourage them to use the kit when they feel upset or stressed.

Tip: Personalize the kit with your child's favorite calming activities.

3. Emotion Regulation Cards:

Purpose: Help children identify and manage their emotions.

Materials: Index cards, markers.

Instructions: Create a set of cards with different emotions and corresponding regulation strategies (e.g., "I feel angry – take deep breaths," "I feel sad – talk to someone"). Use the cards to guide your child in managing their emotions.

Tip: Review the cards regularly and add new strategies as needed.

Real-Life Example

Consider the story of Sophie, a six-year-old girl who struggled with managing her emotions and social interactions. Her parents, Jennifer and Mark, decided to implement practical activities to foster her emotional growth. They created an emotion wheel to help Sophie identify her feelings and a calm down kit for moments of stress. They also engaged in cooperative games and role-playing to improve her social skills. Over time, Sophie became more adept at expressing her emotions, managing stress, and interacting positively with her peers. These activities significantly contributed to her emotional development and well-being.

Reflection Questions

1. Which activities does your child enjoy the most?

2. How can you incorporate more playtime into your child's daily routine?

3. In what ways can you participate in your child's play to strengthen your bond and support their emotional development?

Conclusion

Practical activities play a crucial role in fostering emotional growth in children. By engaging in these activities, parents and educators can help children develop emotional awareness, empathy, social skills, and emotional regulation. Remember, each child is unique, and it is essential to adapt these activities to fit their individual needs and interests.

As we continue this journey through the book, we will explore more strategies and techniques to nurture your child's emotional development. Embrace the power of practical activities and watch as your child grows into a resilient, empathetic, and well-rounded individual.

Maria Montessori: "Play is the work of the child."

[Maria Montessori, renowned educator and creator of the Montessori method, highlights the essential role of play in children's development. This quote aligns with the theme of using practical activities to foster emotional growth, emphasizing that through play, children learn and develop emotionally.]

Viktor Frankl: "Between stimulus and response, there is a space. In that space is our power to choose our response. In our response lies our growth and our freedom."

[Viktor Frankl, psychiatrist and Holocaust survivor, emphasizes the importance of mindful reflection and choice in personal growth. This quote resonates with the theme of fostering emotional growth through activities that encourage children to pause, reflect, and choose their responses wisely.]

Chapter 10

Inculcating Values and Providing Purpose

Introduction

Values and a sense of purpose are foundational to a child's emotional and moral development. They guide behaviour, shape character, and provide a sense of direction in life. Inculcating values and providing purpose helps children understand what is important, make ethical decisions, and find meaning in their actions and experiences.

In this chapter, we will explore the importance of inculcating values and providing a sense of purpose for children. We will discuss practical strategies for teaching values, ways to help children discover their purpose, and the long-term benefits of these efforts. By embedding values and purpose into everyday life, parents and educators can support children in becoming compassionate, responsible, and fulfilled individuals.

The Importance of Values and Purpose

Values are the principles and standards that guide behaviour. They are taught through example, instruction, and experience. A sense of purpose provides children with a reason for their actions and a direction for their efforts. Together, values and purpose contribute to:

1. Moral Development: Helping children distinguish between right and wrong and make ethical choices.

2. Emotional Well-Being: Providing a sense of stability and security by knowing what is important and meaningful.

3. Social Responsibility: Encouraging children to contribute positively to their communities and the world.

4. Personal Fulfillment: Helping children find joy and satisfaction in their endeavors and relationships.

Practical Strategies for Teaching Values

1. Modelling Values:

    Purpose: Demonstrate the values you wish to instill in your children through your actions and words.

    Example: Show respect, kindness, and honesty in your interactions with others.

    Tip: Be mindful of your behaviour, as children often emulate the adults they look up to.

2. Family Discussions:

    Purpose: Engage in conversations about values and their importance.

    Example: Discuss scenarios and ask your child what they would do and why.

    Tip: Use current events, books, or personal experiences as conversation starters.

3. Storytelling:

    Purpose: Use stories to illustrate values and moral lessons.

    Example: Share fables, folktales, or personal anecdotes that highlight key values.

    Tip: After the story, discuss the moral and how it applies to real-life situations.

4. Value-Based Activities:

   Purpose: Reinforce values through structured activities and projects.

   Example: Volunteer as a family, participate in community service, or create a kindness calendar.

   Tip: Reflect on these activities and discuss the values they represent.

5. Positive Reinforcement:

   Purpose: Encourage and reward behaviours that align with your family's values.

   Example: Praise your child for acts of kindness, honesty, or responsibility.

   Tip: Be specific about your praise, such as, "I appreciate how honest you were about what happened at school today."

Helping Children Discover Their Purpose

1. Encouraging Interests and Passions:

   Purpose: Help children explore their interests and passions to find what brings them joy and fulfillment.

   Example: Provide opportunities for your child to try different activities, such as sports, arts, or science projects.

   Tip: Support your child's interests and encourage them to pursue what they love.

2. Setting Goals:

   Purpose: Teach children to set and achieve goals, fostering a sense of purpose and accomplishment.

   Example: Help your child set short-term and long-term goals, and celebrate their progress.

   Tip: Use a goal chart to track achievements and provide motivation.

3. Fostering a Growth Mindset:

   Purpose: Encourage children to view challenges as opportunities for growth and learning.

   Example: Praise effort and perseverance rather than just outcomes.

   Tip: Use phrases like, "You worked really hard on this," to emphasize the value of effort.

4. Connecting to Community:

   Purpose: Help children understand their role in the larger community and the impact they can have.

   Example: Participate in community events, volunteer together, or join local groups.

   Tip: Discuss how their actions contribute to the well-being of others.

5. Reflecting on Experiences:

   Purpose: Encourage children to reflect on their experiences and what they have learned.

Example: Ask questions like, "What did you enjoy most about this activity?" and "What did you learn about yourself?"

Tip: Use a journal or drawing activity to help your child express their reflections.

Long-Term Benefits of Inculcating Values and Purpose

1. Stronger Character:

    Children with strong values and a sense of purpose develop a robust moral character. They are more likely to make ethical decisions and act with integrity.

    Example: A child who values honesty will choose to tell the truth, even when it is difficult.

2. Enhanced Resilience:

    Values and purpose provide a foundation for resilience. Children are better equipped to handle challenges and setbacks with a clear sense of what is important.

    Example: A child with a purpose-driven mindset will persist in the face of obstacles, knowing their efforts are meaningful.

3. Improved Relationships:

    Values such as empathy, respect, and kindness lead to healthier and more fulfilling relationships.

Example: A child who values empathy will be more considerate and understanding in their interactions with others.

4. Greater Life Satisfaction:

    A sense of purpose contributes to overall life satisfaction and well-being. Children who understand their purpose are more likely to feel fulfilled and content.

    Example: A child who finds purpose in helping others will derive joy and satisfaction from their actions.

5. Positive Impact on Society:

    Values-driven individuals contribute positively to their communities and society as a whole. They are more likely to engage in pro-social behaviours and work towards the common good.

    Example: A child who values social responsibility may volunteer, advocate for causes, or take on leadership roles.

Real-Life Example

Consider the story of Aisha, a ten-year-old girl who exhibited strong values and a clear sense of purpose. Her parents, Farah and Ahmed, regularly engaged in family discussions about honesty, respect, and kindness. They encouraged Aisha to pursue her passion for art and supported her involvement in community service projects. Aisha set goals for her artwork and participated in local art fairs to raise funds for charity. Over time, Aisha developed a strong moral character, resilience, and a deep sense of fulfillment. Her values and purpose-driven mindset guided her actions and positively impacted those around her.

Reflection Questions

1. What values are most important to you and your family?

2. How can you instill these values in your child's daily life?

3. What activities can you engage in to help your child discover their purpose?

Conclusion

Inculcating values and providing a sense of purpose are essential for a child's emotional and moral development. By teaching values through modeling, discussions, storytelling, and activities, parents and educators can guide children towards becoming compassionate, responsible, and fulfilled individuals. Helping children discover their purpose through exploration, goal-setting, and community involvement fosters a sense of direction and meaning in their lives.

As we continue this journey through the book, we will explore more strategies and techniques to nurture your child's emotional development. Embrace the power of values and purpose, and watch as your child grows into a morally strong, resilient, and purpose-driven individual.

———◆◆———

Mahatma Gandhi: "The best way to find yourself is to lose yourself in the service of others."

[Mahatma Gandhi, a leader of India's independence movement and a global symbol of peace and nonviolence, emphasizes the profound sense of purpose and fulfillment that comes from serving others. This quote aligns with the theme of inculcating values and providing purpose, highlighting the importance of altruism and selflessness.]

Albert Schweitzer: "The purpose of human life is to serve, and to show compassion and the will to help others."

[Albert Schweitzer, a theologian, philosopher, and Nobel Peace Prize laureate, underscores the significance of compassion and service as fundamental values. This quote resonates with the theme of guiding children to find purpose and instill values that emphasize empathy and helping others.]

Chapter 11

The Collaborative Role of Family

Introduction

Family is the first and most influential environment where a child learns about relationships, values, and emotional dynamics. The collaborative role of the family in a child's development cannot be overstated. When family members work together to provide a supportive, nurturing environment, they foster emotional growth, resilience, and well-being in children.

In this chapter, we will explore the importance of family collaboration, the roles of different family members, and practical strategies for fostering a collaborative family environment. By understanding and embracing the collaborative role of family, parents and caregivers can create a strong foundation for a child's emotional and social development.

The Importance of Family Collaboration

Family collaboration involves working together to support each other's needs, creating a harmonious and nurturing environment. The benefits of family collaboration include:

1. Emotional Support:

    Family members provide a secure base for children to express their emotions and seek comfort.

    Example: A child feels safe sharing their fears and worries with family members, knowing they will be met with understanding and support.

2. Role Modeling:

    Children learn by observing family members' behaviours, interactions, and problem-solving skills.

    Example: Parents who model respectful communication and conflict resolution teach their children how to handle interpersonal challenges.

3. Consistency and Stability:

   A collaborative family environment offers consistent values, rules, and routines, which are crucial for a child's sense of security.

   Example: Regular family meals, bedtime routines, and shared activities create a predictable and comforting structure for children.

4. Enhanced Communication:

   Open and honest communication within the family helps address issues and strengthens relationships.

   Example: Family meetings provide a platform for discussing concerns, planning activities, and making decisions together.

5. Shared Responsibility:

   Collaborative families share responsibilities, ensuring that everyone contributes to the household and supports each other.

   Example: Assigning age-appropriate chores helps children learn responsibility and teamwork.

Roles of Different Family Members

1. Parents:

   Role: Primary caregivers and role models who provide guidance, support, and love.

Responsibilities: Establishing rules, offering emotional support, modeling positive behaviour, and fostering a nurturing environment.

2. Siblings:

    Role: Companions and peers who influence social skills and provide mutual support.

    Responsibilities: Building positive relationships, sharing responsibilities, and offering emotional support to each other.

3. Extended Family Members:

    Role: Additional sources of support, wisdom, and cultural continuity.

    Responsibilities: Providing care and guidance, sharing family traditions, and offering emotional and practical support.

4. Grandparents:

    Role: Sources of love, wisdom, and stability.

    Responsibilities: Offering emotional support, sharing life experiences, and maintaining family traditions.

Practical Strategies for Fostering a Collaborative Family Environment

1. Family Meetings:

    Purpose: Facilitate open communication and collective decision-making.

Implementation: Schedule regular family meetings to discuss plans, address concerns, and celebrate achievements.

Tip: Encourage all family members to participate and share their thoughts.

2. Shared Activities:

Purpose: Strengthen family bonds and create positive shared experiences.

Implementation: Plan activities that everyone can enjoy, such as game nights, outdoor adventures, or creative projects.

Tip: Rotate activity planning to include everyone's interests and preferences.

3. Chore Rotation:

Purpose: Teach responsibility and teamwork.

Implementation: Create a chore chart that assigns age-appropriate tasks to each family member and rotates responsibilities regularly.

Tip: Use positive reinforcement to acknowledge and reward contributions.

4. Open Communication:

Purpose: Foster a culture of honesty and trust.

Implementation: Encourage family members to express their feelings and thoughts openly, and listen actively to each other.

Tip: Practice reflective listening by paraphrasing what others say to show understanding and empathy.

5. Problem-Solving Together:

Purpose: Develop collaborative problem-solving skills.

Implementation: Address family challenges by brainstorming solutions together and agreeing on a plan of action.

Tip: Use a problem-solving framework, such as identifying the problem, generating options, evaluating solutions, and implementing the best one.

6. Celebrating Achievements:

Purpose: Build self-esteem and a sense of accomplishment.

Implementation: Recognize and celebrate individual and family achievements, both big and small.

Tip: Create a family achievement board where accomplishments are displayed and celebrated.

Real-Life Example

Consider the story of the Ramirez family. Maria and Carlos, along with their children, Diego and Sofia, faced the challenge of balancing busy work and school schedules while maintaining a strong family bond. They decided to implement regular family meetings to discuss their plans and address any issues. They also established a chore rotation system and planned weekly family activities, such as hiking and cooking together.

By fostering a collaborative environment, the Ramirez family strengthened their communication, built stronger relationships, and created a supportive and nurturing home for Diego and Sofia.

Reflection Questions

1. How does your family currently collaborate to support each other?

2. What strategies can you implement to improve family collaboration and communication?

3. How can you involve all family members in creating a supportive and nurturing environment?

Conclusion

The collaborative role of the family is essential for a child's emotional and social development. By working together, family members can create a nurturing environment that fosters emotional support, role modeling, consistency, and open communication. Practical strategies such as family meetings, shared activities, chore rotations, and problem-solving together can strengthen family bonds and support a child's growth.

As we continue this journey through the book, we will explore more strategies and techniques to nurture your child's emotional development. Embrace the power of family collaboration and watch as your child thrives in a loving and supportive environment.

Barbara Coloroso: "If kids come to us from strong, healthy functioning families, it makes our job easier. If they do not come to us from strong, healthy, functioning families, it makes our job more important."

[Barbara Coloroso, educator and parenting expert, highlights the critical role that families play in the development and well-being of children. This quote resonates with the theme of family collaboration, stressing the importance of a supportive family environment in nurturing a child's growth.]

Desmond Tutu: "You don't choose your family. They are God's gift to you, as you are to them."

[Desmond Tutu, Nobel Peace Prize laureate and human rights activist, underscores the inherent value and importance of family bonds. This quote aligns with the theme of the collaborative role of family, emphasizing the mutual support and unique connection that families provide.]

Chapter 12

Balancing Physical Development and Emotional Well-Being

Introduction

Physical development and emotional well-being are closely interconnected aspects of a child's overall growth. A balanced approach that nurtures both physical health and emotional resilience is essential for a child's holistic development. Understanding how physical activities and emotional health influence each other can help parents and educators create environments that support and enhance both.

In this chapter, we will explore the relationship between physical development and emotional well-being. We will discuss practical strategies to promote physical health and emotional resilience, offering valuable insights for fostering a balanced and healthy lifestyle for children.

The Connection Between Physical Development and Emotional Well-Being

Physical development and emotional well-being are interdependent. Physical activity and health directly impact a child's emotional state, while emotional well-being influences physical health and performance. Key connections include:

1. Exercise and Mood:

    Physical activity releases endorphins, which improve mood and reduce stress.

    Example: Children who engage in regular physical exercise often exhibit higher levels of happiness and lower levels of anxiety.

2. Sleep and Emotional Regulation:

    Adequate sleep is crucial for emotional regulation and cognitive function.

Example: Children who get enough sleep are better able to manage their emotions and concentrate in school.

3. Nutrition and Behaviour:

    A balanced diet supports physical health and influences behaviour and emotional stability.

    Example: Proper nutrition can improve focus, reduce hyperactivity, and stabilize mood swings.

4. Body Awareness and Self-Esteem:

    Physical activities that promote body awareness contribute to a positive self-image and self-esteem.

    Example: Participating in sports or dance can help children feel more confident and capable.

Practical Strategies for Promoting Physical Health

1. Encouraging Regular Exercise:

    Purpose: Support physical development and emotional well-being through regular physical activity.

    Activities: Sports, dance, swimming, biking, yoga.

    Tip: Find activities that your child enjoys and incorporate them into a routine.

2. Ensuring Adequate Sleep:

    Purpose: Promote emotional regulation and cognitive function through sufficient sleep.

Strategies: Establish a consistent bedtime routine, create a calming sleep environment, limit screen time before bed.

Tip: Encourage relaxation techniques such as reading or listening to calming music before bedtime.

3. Providing Balanced Nutrition:

Purpose: Support overall health and emotional stability through proper nutrition.

Strategies: Offer a variety of fruits, vegetables, whole grains, and lean proteins. Limit sugary snacks and drinks.

Tip: Involve your child in meal planning and preparation to encourage healthy eating habits.

4. Promoting Outdoor Activities:

Purpose: Enhance physical health and emotional well-being through outdoor play.

Activities: Hiking, playing in the park, gardening, nature walks.

Tip: Plan regular family outings to natural settings to encourage a connection with nature.

5. Encouraging Hydration:

Purpose: Maintain physical health and cognitive function through proper hydration.

Strategies: Ensure your child drinks enough water throughout the day.

Tip: Provide a reusable water bottle and encourage regular water breaks.

Practical Strategies for Promoting Emotional Well-Being

1. Mindfulness and Relaxation Techniques:

    Purpose: Enhance emotional regulation and reduce stress through mindfulness practices.

    Activities: Deep breathing, meditation, progressive muscle relaxation.

    Tip: Practice mindfulness together as a family to model and encourage these techniques.

2. Building Emotional Awareness:

    Purpose: Help children recognize and articulate their emotions.

    Activities: Emotion wheel, feelings journal, emotion charades.

    Tip: Regularly discuss emotions and validate your child's feelings.

3. Creating a Supportive Environment:

    Purpose: Foster a sense of security and well-being through a nurturing environment.

    Strategies: Provide consistent routines, offer emotional support, encourage open communication.

Tip: Create a "safe space" at home where your child can retreat and relax when needed.

4. Encouraging Positive Relationships:

    Purpose: Support emotional well-being through healthy social connections.

    Activities: Playdates, family activities, group sports or clubs.

    Tip: Teach social skills such as empathy, active listening, and conflict resolution.

5. Setting Realistic Goals:

    Purpose: Promote a sense of purpose and accomplishment through goal-setting.

    Strategies: Help your child set achievable short-term and long-term goals.

    Tip: Celebrate progress and achievements to build confidence and motivation.

Integrating Physical and Emotional Well-Being

1. Family Activities:

    Purpose: Foster physical health and emotional connections through shared activities.

    Activities: Family walks, biking, cooking healthy meals together, yoga sessions.

Tip: Make physical activities a regular part of family life to model a balanced lifestyle.

2. Active Play:

Purpose: Support physical development and emotional expression through active play.

Activities: Tag, obstacle courses, dance parties, sports.

Tip: Encourage free play and join in to strengthen family bonds and have fun together.

3. Mindful Movement:

Purpose: Combine physical activity with mindfulness to promote holistic well-being.

Activities: Yoga, tai chi, mindful walking.

Tip: Practice mindful movement together, focusing on breathing and body awareness.

4. Balanced Routines:

Purpose: Create a balanced daily routine that incorporates physical activity, rest, and emotional check-ins.

Strategies: Schedule time for exercise, relaxation, and family discussions about emotions.

Tip: Adjust routines as needed to ensure a healthy balance and accommodate your child's needs.

Real-Life Example

Consider the story of Jack, a nine-year-old boy who struggled with anxiety and poor physical health. His parents, Sarah and Tom, decided to take a holistic approach to improve both his physical and emotional well-being. They incorporated regular family hikes, encouraged Jack to join a soccer team, and established a consistent bedtime routine. They also practiced mindfulness exercises together and created a supportive home environment where Jack felt safe discussing his feelings. Over time, Jack's physical health improved, and he became more emotionally resilient and confident. The balanced approach significantly enhanced his overall well-being.

Reflection Questions

1. How do physical activities influence your child's emotional well-being?

2. What steps can you take to ensure your child gets enough exercise, sleep, and proper nutrition?

3. How can you integrate physical and emotional well-being practices into your family's daily routine?

Conclusion

Balancing physical development and emotional well-being is essential for a child's overall growth and happiness. By promoting regular exercise, adequate sleep, balanced nutrition, and emotional awareness, parents and educators can create a nurturing environment that supports holistic development. Integrating physical and emotional well-being practices into daily routines fosters resilience, confidence, and a positive outlook on life.

As we continue this journey through the book, we will explore more strategies and techniques to nurture your child's emotional development. Embrace the interconnectedness of physical health and emotional well-being, and watch as your child thrives in a balanced and supportive environment.

Hippocrates: "If we could give every individual the right amount of nourishment and exercise, not too little and not too much, we would have found the safest way to health."

[Hippocrates, the ancient Greek physician known as the "Father of Medicine," highlights the importance of balance in physical health. This quote aligns with the theme of balancing physical development and emotional well-being, emphasizing the need for moderation and care in nurturing overall health.]

Thich Nhat Hanh: "To keep the body in good health is a duty... otherwise we shall not be able to keep our mind strong and clear."

[Thich Nhat Hanh, a renowned Buddhist monk and peace activist, underscores the connection between physical health and mental clarity. This quote resonates with the theme of integrating physical activities and emotional well-being, stressing that taking care of the body is essential for maintaining a healthy mind.]

Chapter 13

Understanding and Addressing Learning Disabilities

Introduction

Learning disabilities can pose significant challenges for children, impacting their academic performance, self-esteem, and emotional well-being. These disabilities, which include dyslexia, dysgraphia, dyscalculia, Attention

Deficit Disorder (ADD), and Attention Deficit Hyperactivity Disorder (ADHD), require targeted strategies and support to help affected children succeed.

In this chapter, we will explore the different types of learning disabilities, their characteristics, and practical strategies for addressing them. By understanding and effectively addressing learning disabilities, parents and educators can provide the necessary support to help children overcome challenges and reach their full potential.

Types of Learning Disabilities

Learning disabilities are neurological disorders that affect a child's ability to process information. They can manifest in various forms, including difficulties with reading, writing, and math.

1. Dyslexia:

    Description: A reading disability characterized by difficulty with accurate and/or fluent word recognition and poor spelling abilities.

    Symptoms: Trouble reading words, slow reading rate, difficulty with spelling, and issues with phonological processing.

2. Dysgraphia:

    Description: A writing disability that affects handwriting, spelling, and the ability to organize thoughts on paper.

Symptoms: Illegible handwriting, inconsistent spacing, poor spelling, and difficulty composing written text.

3. Dyscalculia:

    Description: A math disability that affects the ability to understand numbers and learn math facts.

    Symptoms: Difficulty with number sense, calculation, understanding math concepts, and remembering math facts.

4. Attention Deficit Disorder (ADD):

    Description: A disorder characterized by inattention, distractibility, and poor organizational skills without the hyperactivity component.

    Symptoms: Trouble focusing, forgetfulness, disorganization, and difficulty following instructions.

5. Attention Deficit Hyperactivity Disorder (ADHD):

    Description: A disorder that includes symptoms of inattention, hyperactivity, and impulsivity.

    Symptoms: Fidgeting, difficulty staying seated, excessive talking, interrupting others, and trouble focusing.

Understanding the Impact of Learning Disabilities

Learning disabilities can affect various aspects of a child's life, including:

1. Academic Performance:

   Struggles with reading, writing, and math can lead to poor grades and frustration.

   Example: A child with dyslexia may fall behind in reading comprehension, affecting their overall academic progress.

2. Self-Esteem:

   Consistent difficulties and failures can damage a child's self-esteem and confidence.

   Example: A child with dysgraphia may feel embarrassed about their handwriting and reluctant to participate in writing activities.

3. Social Interactions:

   Learning disabilities can impact social skills and peer relationships.

   Example: A child with ADHD may struggle to maintain friendships due to impulsive behaviours.

4. Emotional Well-Being:

   The stress and frustration of dealing with learning disabilities can lead to anxiety, depression, and behavioural issues.

   Example: A child with dyscalculia may experience anxiety during math lessons and tests.

Practical Strategies for Addressing Learning Disabilities

1. Dyslexia:

Multisensory Instruction:

Purpose: Engage multiple senses to enhance reading skills.

Strategies: Use visual, auditory, and kinesthetic activities to teach phonics and reading.

Tip: Incorporate tools like sandpaper letters, audiobooks, and letter tiles.

Reading Programs:

Purpose: Provide structured reading interventions.

Strategies: Use evidence-based reading programs designed for dyslexia, such as Orton-Gillingham or Wilson Reading System.

Tip: Work with a specialized reading tutor if possible.

Assistive Technology:

Purpose: Support reading and writing through technology.

Strategies: Use text-to-speech software, audiobooks, and spellcheck tools.

Tip: Encourage the use of apps that support reading comprehension.

2. Dysgraphia:

    Fine Motor Skill Activities:

    Purpose: Improve handwriting and coordination.

    Strategies: Engage in activities that strengthen hand muscles, such as drawing, cutting, and playing with clay.

    Tip: Use specialized grips or adaptive pencils.

    Writing Assistance:

    Purpose: Support written expression.

    Strategies: Use graphic organizers, sentence starters, and word prediction software.

    Tip: Encourage typing on a computer to reduce the strain of handwriting.

    Explicit Instruction:

    Purpose: Teach writing skills systematically.

    Strategies: Break writing tasks into smaller steps and provide clear, step-by-step instructions.

    Tip: Use visual aids and checklists to guide the writing process.

3. Dyscalculia:

    Concrete-Representational-Abstract (CRA) Approach:

    Purpose: Enhance understanding of math concepts.

Strategies: Start with concrete manipulatives, move to representational drawings, and then to abstract symbols.

Tip: Use tools like counting blocks, number lines, and visual aids.

Math Games:

Purpose: Make math practice engaging and fun.

Strategies: Use games and apps that reinforce math skills in an interactive way.

Tip: Incorporate everyday math activities, such as cooking or shopping, to practice skills in real-life contexts.

Step-by-Step Instruction:

Purpose: Simplify complex math tasks.

Strategies: Break down math problems into smaller, manageable steps and provide clear instructions.

Tip: Use visual aids and math journals to track steps and solutions.

4. ADD:

Organizational Tools:

Purpose: Improve focus and organization.

Strategies: Use planners, checklists, and timers to help manage tasks and time.

Tip: Teach prioritization and time-management skills.

Environmental Adjustments:

Purpose: Minimize distractions.

Strategies: Create a quiet, clutter-free workspace with minimal distractions.

Tip: Use noise-canceling headphones or background music to aid concentration.

Behavioural Interventions:

Purpose: Reinforce positive behaviours.

Strategies: Use reward systems, positive reinforcement, and clear expectations.

Tip: Set specific, achievable goals and celebrate progress.

5. ADHD:

Behavioural Strategies:

Purpose: Manage hyperactivity and impulsivity.

Strategies: Implement behaviour charts, token systems, and consistent routines.

Tip: Use visual schedules and reminders to provide structure.

Physical Activity:

Purpose: Channel excess energy constructively.

Strategies: Incorporate regular physical activities, such as sports or exercise breaks, throughout the day.

Tip: Use movement-based learning activities to engage the body and mind.

Mindfulness and Relaxation:

Purpose: Improve focus and self-regulation.

Strategies: Teach mindfulness practices, such as deep breathing, meditation, and yoga.

Tip: Practice mindfulness together as a family to model and reinforce these techniques.

Cultural Sensitivity in Addressing Learning Disabilities

Cultural context significantly influences how learning disabilities are perceived and managed. Incorporating cultural sensitivity is crucial in effectively addressing these issues.

Understand Cultural Norms:

Recognize and respect the cultural values and norms of the child's family.

Avoid imposing one's own cultural expectations and practices.

Example: Learn about the family's cultural background and incorporate culturally relevant practices into interventions.

Incorporate Cultural Practices:

Use culturally relevant examples and practices in interventions and activities.

Include traditional coping mechanisms and support systems, such as community elders or spiritual leaders.

Example: Integrate cultural rituals and practices into therapy sessions to make the child feel more comfortable.

Engage with the Community:

Involve community leaders and cultural advisors in supporting gifted children.

Utilize community resources such as cultural centers and support groups to provide additional support.

Example: Partner with local cultural organizations to create programs that support the child's emotional development.

Adapt Communication Styles:

Be mindful of different communication styles and preferences based on cultural backgrounds.

Use language that is respectful and inclusive of the child's cultural context.

Example: Use bilingual materials and involve cultural liaisons to facilitate effective communication.

Collaborative Approaches

1. Working with Teachers:

    Purpose: Ensure consistent support at school.

    Strategies: Communicate regularly with teachers, share information about your child's needs, and collaborate on individualized education plans (IEPs).

    Tip: Attend parent-teacher meetings and advocate for necessary accommodations.

2. Seeking Professional Help:

    Purpose: Access specialized support.

    Strategies: Consult with educational psychologists, speech therapists, and occupational therapists as needed.

    Tip: Explore therapy options that address specific learning disabilities, such as cognitive-behavioural therapy (CBT), for anxiety related to learning challenges.

3. Support Groups:

    Purpose: Connect with others who understand similar challenges.

    Strategies: Join support groups for parents and children dealing with learning disabilities.

    Tip: Participate in group activities and share experiences and strategies.

Real-Life Example

Consider the case of Juan, an eight-year-old boy diagnosed with dyslexia. His parents, Maria and Carlos, noticed his struggles with reading and writing and sought help from his teacher, Ms. Rivera, who worked with them to create a supportive and culturally sensitive environment.

Ms. Rivera implemented multisensory teaching methods in her classroom, using activities that engaged Juan's visual, auditory, and kinesthetic-tactile senses. She also recommended assistive technology tools such as text-to-speech software to aid Juan's reading.

Maria and Carlos involved Juan in community programs that emphasized reading and literacy, providing him with additional support and encouragement. They also sought advice from cultural advisors to ensure the interventions were respectful of their cultural values.

Over time, Juan's reading skills improved, and he became more confident in his abilities. The collaborative and culturally sensitive approach helped Juan overcome his learning disability and thrive academically.

Reflection Questions

1. What learning disabilities does your child face, and how do they impact their academic and emotional well-being?

2. Which strategies discussed in this chapter can you implement to support your child's learning and development?

3. How can you collaborate with teachers and professionals to create a comprehensive support plan for your child?

Conclusion

Understanding and addressing learning disabilities is crucial for a child's academic success and emotional well-being. By implementing targeted strategies, collaborating with educators and professionals, and fostering a supportive home environment, parents and caregivers can help children overcome learning challenges and reach their full potential. Embrace the journey of supporting your child's unique learning needs, and watch as they grow into confident, resilient, and capable individuals.

As we continue this journey through the book, we will explore more strategies and techniques to nurture your child's emotional development. Embrace the power of understanding and addressing learning disabilities, and watch as your child thrives in a supportive and nurturing environment.

———◆◆———

Albert Einstein: "Everybody is a genius. But if you judge a fish by its ability to climb a tree, it will live its whole life believing that it is stupid."

[Albert Einstein, theoretical physicist and Nobel laureate, highlights the importance of recognizing and valuing individual strengths and differences. This quote aligns with the theme of understanding

and addressing learning disabilities by emphasizing the need to appreciate each child's unique abilities.]

Louisa May Alcott: "I am not afraid of storms, for I am learning how to sail my ship."

[Louisa May Alcott, acclaimed author of "Little Women," speaks to the resilience and perseverance required to overcome challenges. This quote resonates with the theme of supporting children with learning disabilities, encouraging them to navigate and conquer their difficulties with determination and support.]

Chapter 14

Nurturing Gifted Children

Introduction

Gifted children often exhibit advanced intellectual, creative, or artistic abilities compared to their peers. While these talents can be a source of great pride and potential, they also come with unique challenges. Nurturing gifted children requires a balanced approach that fosters their exceptional abilities while addressing their emotional and social needs.

In this chapter, we will explore the characteristics of gifted children, the challenges they face, and practical strategies for supporting their development. By understanding and meeting the needs of gifted children, parents and educators can help them reach their full potential while maintaining a healthy and balanced life.

Characteristics of Gifted Children

Gifted children display advanced abilities and talents in one or more areas, such as intellectual, creative, artistic, or leadership skills. Recognizing and understanding these abilities is crucial for providing appropriate support and nurturing their development. Gifted children may display a range of characteristics, including:

1. Intellectual Abilities:

    Advanced reasoning, problem-solving skills, and an insatiable curiosity.

    Example: A child who reads at an advanced level and shows a deep interest in complex subjects.

2. Creative Abilities:

    Original thinking, creativity, and a strong imagination.

    Example: A child who excels in artistic endeavors or comes up with innovative solutions to problems.

3. Emotional Sensitivity:

    Heightened emotional awareness, empathy, and sensitivity.

    Example: A child who is deeply affected by social issues or shows strong compassion for others.

4. Intense Focus:

    The ability to concentrate deeply on interests and activities.

    Example: A child who becomes absorbed in a hobby or subject for extended periods.

5. High Energy Levels:

    Enthusiasm and high energy, which can sometimes be mistaken for hyperactivity.

    Example: A child who is constantly engaged in activities and eager to explore new things.

Challenges Faced by Gifted Children

Gifted children may encounter several challenges, including:

1. Perfectionism:

    The desire to achieve perfection can lead to anxiety and fear of failure.

    Example: A child who becomes frustrated or discouraged when their work is not flawless.

2. Boredom:

   Gifted children may become bored with standard curricula and activities.

   Example: A child who finishes assignments quickly and then disrupts the class due to lack of engagement.

3. Social Isolation:

   Differences in interests and abilities can make it challenging to connect with peers.

   Example: A child who struggles to find friends with similar intellectual or creative interests.

4. Emotional Intensity:

   Heightened emotions can lead to intense reactions and mood swings.

   Example: A child who experiences strong emotional responses to everyday situations.

5. Pressure to Succeed:

   High expectations from themselves and others can create significant stress.

   Example: A child who feels pressured to excel academically and meet the expectations of parents and teachers.

Practical Strategies for Nurturing Gifted Children

To effectively support gifted children, it is essential to implement strategies that are detailed, practical, and culturally sensitive.

1. Differentiated Instruction:

    Purpose: Tailor education to meet the individual needs of gifted children.

    Strategies: Provide advanced materials, enrichment activities, and opportunities for independent study.

    Tip: Work with teachers to develop a personalized learning plan that challenges and engages your child.

2. Encouraging Creativity:

    Purpose: Foster creative expression and original thinking.

    Activities: Provide opportunities for artistic pursuits, creative writing, and problem-solving projects.

    Tip: Create a supportive environment where creative ideas are valued and encouraged.

3. Supporting Emotional Needs:

    Purpose: Address the emotional sensitivity and intensity of gifted children.

    Strategies: Teach emotional regulation techniques, provide a safe space for expressing feelings, and encourage open communication.

Tip: Validate your child's emotions and help them develop healthy coping strategies.

4. Facilitating Social Connections:

    Purpose: Help gifted children build meaningful relationships with peers.

    Activities: Enroll your child in clubs, groups, or classes that align with their interests and abilities.

    Tip: Encourage participation in activities where they can meet like-minded peers and form lasting friendships.

5. Balancing Challenges and Support:

    Purpose: Provide appropriate challenges while offering support and guidance.

    Strategies: Set realistic goals, offer encouragement, and celebrate achievements.

    Tip: Help your child understand that it is okay to make mistakes, and that learning is a continuous process.

6. Managing Perfectionism:

    Purpose: Help children cope with perfectionism and reduce anxiety.

    Strategies: Encourage a growth mindset, emphasize effort over results, and model healthy attitudes towards failure.

    Tip: Share stories of famous individuals who have learned from their mistakes and achieved success.

7. Providing Enrichment Opportunities:

    Purpose: Offer additional learning experiences beyond the standard curriculum.

    Activities: Enroll your child in summer programs, workshops, and extracurricular activities that align with their interests.

    Tip: Look for programs that offer hands-on, experiential learning opportunities.

Cultural Sensitivity in Nurturing Gifted Children

Cultural context significantly influences how giftedness is perceived and nurtured. Incorporating cultural sensitivity is crucial in effectively supporting these children.

1. Recognize Cultural Differences:

    Understand that cultural values and norms can impact how giftedness is expressed and perceived.

    Example: Some cultures may prioritize collective success over individual achievement.

2. Incorporate Cultural Practices:

    Use culturally relevant examples and practices in interventions and activities.

    Example: Integrating cultural heritage projects into the curriculum to celebrate diversity.

3. Engage with the Community:

    Involve community leaders and cultural advisors in supporting gifted children.

    Example: Partnering with cultural organizations to provide enrichment activities and resources.

4. Adapt Communication Styles:

    Be mindful of different communication styles and preferences based on cultural backgrounds.

    Example: Using culturally appropriate language and considering cultural norms when discussing the child's abilities and needs.

Real-Life Example

Consider the case of Amina, a ten-year-old girl recognized for her exceptional abilities in mathematics and science. Her parents, Samir and Leila, noticed her boredom and frustration with the standard curriculum and sought help from her school.

Amina's teacher, Ms. Patel, collaborated with Samir and Leila to develop an individualized education plan (IEP) that included subject acceleration for mathematics and science. Ms. Patel also recommended enrolling Amina in a local science club where she could interact with peers who shared her interests.

To address Amina's emotional needs, Ms. Patel introduced mindfulness exercises and encouraged open discussions about her feelings. Samir and Leila also involved Amina in cultural activities and heritage projects to celebrate her background and foster a sense of belonging.

Over time, Amina's academic performance and emotional well-being improved significantly. The collaborative and culturally sensitive approach helped Amina thrive and fully embrace her giftedness.

Reflection Questions

1.   What are your child's unique gifts and talents?

2.   How can you provide opportunities for your child to explore and develop these abilities?

3.   What strategies can you implement to support your child's emotional and social needs?

Conclusion

Nurturing gifted children requires a balanced approach that addresses their intellectual, creative, emotional, and social needs. By providing differentiated instruction, encouraging creativity, supporting emotional well-being, facilitating social connections, and managing perfectionism, parents and educators can help gifted children reach their full potential. Embrace the journey of nurturing your child's gifts and talents, and watch as they grow into confident, well-rounded individuals.

As we continue this journey through the book, we will explore more strategies and techniques to nurture your child's emotional development. Embrace the unique challenges and opportunities of raising a gifted child, and watch as they thrive in a supportive and enriching environment.

Howard Gardner: "Children are not things to be molded, but are people to be unfolded."

[Howard Gardner, a developmental psychologist best known for his theory of multiple intelligences, emphasizes the importance of recognizing and nurturing the unique potential within each child. This quote aligns with the theme of nurturing gifted children by highlighting the need to support their individual growth and talents.]

Plato: "Do not train a child to learn by force or harshness; but direct them to it by what amuses their minds, so that you may be better able to discover with accuracy the peculiar bent of the genius of each."

[Plato, the ancient Greek philosopher, underscores the importance of guiding children through engaging and enjoyable learning experiences. This quote resonates with the theme of nurturing gifted children by advocating for a supportive and stimulating environment that fosters their natural abilities.]

Chapter 15

Technology and Emotional Development

Introduction

Technology is an integral part of modern life, offering countless benefits and opportunities for learning, communication, and entertainment. However, its impact on emotional development, particularly in children, is a topic of growing concern. Balancing technology use with activities that promote emotional well-being is crucial for fostering healthy development.

In this chapter, we will explore the effects of technology on emotional development, the potential risks and benefits, and practical strategies for managing technology use. By understanding and addressing these aspects, parents and educators can help children navigate the digital world while supporting their emotional growth.

The Impact of Technology on Emotional Development

Technology influences various aspects of emotional development, both positively and negatively. Key areas of impact include:

1. Social Interaction:

   Positive: Technology enables children to connect with peers, family, and communities, fostering social bonds and support networks.

   Negative: Excessive screen time can lead to social isolation and hinder face-to-face interactions.

2. Emotional Regulation:

   Positive: Access to educational apps and resources can help children learn about emotions and coping strategies.

   Negative: Overreliance on digital devices can impede the development of self-regulation skills and increase impulsivity.

3. Self-Esteem:

    Positive: Positive feedback and accomplishments in digital games and activities can boost self-esteem.

    Negative: Exposure to unrealistic standards and cyberbullying on social media can harm self-esteem and body image.

4. Attention and Focus:

    Positive: Interactive and engaging educational content can enhance learning and cognitive skills.

    Negative: Rapidly changing stimuli and multitasking with devices can reduce attention span and focus.

Potential Risks and Benefits of Technology

Risks:

1. Addiction:

    Overuse of technology can lead to addictive behaviours, impacting sleep, academic performance, and physical health.

    Example: A child who spends excessive hours playing video games may neglect homework and physical activities.

2. Cyberbullying:

    Online platforms can expose children to bullying and harassment, affecting their emotional well-being.

Example: A child who experiences negative comments on social media may develop anxiety and depression.

3. Privacy Concerns:

Sharing personal information online can pose privacy risks and lead to identity theft or exploitation.

Example: A child who shares too much information on social media may become a target for online predators.

Benefits:

1. Educational Opportunities:

Technology provides access to a wealth of information, interactive learning tools, and educational games.

Example: A child can use educational apps to improve math skills or learn a new language.

2. Communication Skills:

Technology enables children to communicate with others, enhancing language development and social skills.

Example: Video calls with family members can strengthen relationships and improve communication abilities.

3. Creativity and Innovation:

Digital tools and platforms allow children to express creativity through art, music, and writing.

Example: A child can create digital art or compose music using online tools, exploring their creative talents.

Practical Strategies for Managing Technology Use

1. Setting Limits:

    Purpose: Ensure a balanced approach to technology use.

    Strategies: Establish clear rules and time limits for screen time, including breaks and device-free times.

    Tip: Use apps or built-in device features to monitor and control screen time.

2. Encouraging Active Use:

    Purpose: Promote meaningful and productive use of technology.

    Activities: Encourage educational apps, creative tools, and interactive games that support learning and development.

    Tip: Choose age-appropriate content that aligns with your child's interests and educational goals.

3. Modeling Healthy Behaviour:

    Purpose: Set a positive example for technology use.

    Strategies: Demonstrate balanced technology habits, such as limiting screen time and prioritizing face-to-face interactions.

Tip: Create device-free zones or times, such as during meals or family activities.

4. Fostering Open Communication:

    Purpose: Address concerns and promote safe technology use.

    Strategies: Discuss the benefits and risks of technology with your child, encouraging them to share their experiences and feelings.

    Tip: Educate your child about online safety, privacy, and respectful behaviour.

5. Promoting Offline Activities:

    Purpose: Encourage a balanced lifestyle with diverse experiences.

    Activities: Engage your child in physical activities, hobbies, and social interactions that do not involve screens.

    Tip: Plan regular family outings, sports, and creative projects to provide alternatives to screen time.

Real-Life Example

Consider the story of Ethan, a twelve-year-old boy who spent excessive hours playing video games and browsing social media. His parents, Laura and James, noticed that his grades were slipping, and he was becoming increasingly withdrawn. They decided to implement a balanced approach to technology use. They set clear limits on screen time, encouraged Ethan to use educational apps, and involved him in family activities like hiking and cooking. They also had open discussions about online safety and the impact of excessive screen time. Over time, Ethan's academic performance improved, and he became more engaged in offline activities, developing better emotional and social skills.

Reflection Questions

1. How does technology use currently impact your child's emotional development?

2. What strategies can you implement to balance technology use with offline activities?

3. How can you model healthy technology habits for your child?

Conclusion

Balancing technology use with activities that promote emotional well-being is essential for a child's overall development. By setting limits, encouraging active and meaningful use of technology, modeling healthy behaviour, fostering open communication, and promoting offline activities, parents and educators can help children navigate the digital world while supporting their emotional growth. Embrace the benefits of technology while being mindful of its potential risks, and watch as your child thrives in a balanced and supportive environment.

As we continue this journey through the book, we will explore more strategies and techniques to nurture your child's emotional development. Embrace the power of balanced technology use, and watch as your child grows into a well-rounded and emotionally resilient individual.

Sherry Turkle: "We are at the point where we all need to be able to agree on the importance of balance between technology and human interaction. We must think deeply about how we use our devices and the impact they have on our emotional lives."

[Sherry Turkle, a sociologist and psychologist known for her research on the effects of technology on human relationships, emphasizes the need for a balanced approach to technology use. This quote resonates with the theme of balancing technology and emotional development.]

Bill Gates: "Technology is just a tool. In terms of getting the kids working together and motivating them, the teacher is the most important."

[Bill Gates, co-founder of Microsoft and a prominent advocate for education, underscores the role of human interaction and guidance in the effective use of technology. This quote aligns with the theme of integrating technology in ways that enhance, rather than hinder, emotional development.]

Chapter 16

Building Resilience

Introduction

Resilience is the ability to bounce back from adversity, adapt to change, and keep going in the face of challenges. It is a crucial skill for emotional well-being and success in life. Children who develop resilience are better equipped to handle stress, overcome obstacles, and grow into confident, capable adults.

In this chapter, we will explore the importance of resilience, the factors that contribute to its development, and practical strategies for building resilience in children. By fostering resilience, parents and educators can help children navigate life's ups and downs with confidence and strength.

The Importance of Resilience

Resilience is essential for several reasons:

1. Emotional Regulation:

    Resilient children can manage their emotions and stay calm under pressure.

    Example: A child who remains composed and thinks through solutions when facing a difficult test.

2. Problem-Solving Skills:

    Resilience enhances the ability to solve problems and make decisions.

    Example: A child who figures out different ways to approach a challenging math problem.

3. Adaptability:

    Resilient children adapt to new situations and changes more easily.

    Example: A child who adjusts well to a new school or moving to a new city.

4. Self-Esteem:

    Overcoming challenges boosts self-confidence and self-worth.

    Example: A child who feels proud after successfully completing a difficult project.

5. Social Competence:

    Resilient children build stronger relationships and communicate effectively.

    Example: A child who works well in group projects and resolves conflicts with peers.

Factors Contributing to Resilience

Several factors contribute to the development of resilience in children:

1. Supportive Relationships:

    Positive relationships with family, friends, and mentors provide emotional support and a sense of security.

    Example: A close bond with a caring teacher who offers guidance and encouragement.

2. Positive Self-Perception:

    A healthy self-esteem and belief in one's abilities foster resilience.

    Example: A child who recognizes their strengths and feels nfident in their abilities.

3. Problem-Solving Skills:

The ability to think critically and solve problems enhances resilience.

Example: A child who can brainstorm solutions and make decisions independently.

4. Emotional Regulation:

Managing emotions effectively helps children stay calm and focused during challenges.

Example: A child who practices deep breathing to calm down when feeling anxious.

5. Sense of Purpose:

Having goals and a sense of purpose motivates children to persevere.

Example: A child who is passionate about playing an instrument and works hard to improve their skills.

Practical Strategies for Building Resilience

1. Encouraging Independence:

Purpose: Foster self-reliance and confidence.

Strategies: Give children age-appropriate responsibilities and opportunities to make decisions.

Tip: Encourage your child to try new activities and solve problems on their own.

2. Modeling Resilience:

    Purpose: Demonstrate resilient behaviour through your actions.

    Strategies: Show how you handle stress and setbacks with a positive attitude.

    Tip: Share stories of times when you faced challenges and overcame them.

3. Teaching Problem-Solving Skills:

    Purpose: Enhance critical thinking and decision-making abilities.

    Strategies: Guide children through the process of identifying problems, brainstorming solutions, and evaluating outcomes.

    Tip: Use real-life scenarios to practice problem-solving together.

4. Promoting Emotional Awareness:

    Purpose: Help children recognize and manage their emotions.

    Strategies: Use tools like emotion wheels and feelings journals to discuss emotions.

    Tip: Encourage your child to talk about their feelings and validate their experiences.

5. Fostering a Growth Mindset:

    Purpose: Cultivate a positive attitude towards challenges and learning.

Strategies: Praise effort and perseverance rather than just results.

Tip: Use phrases like, "You worked really hard on this," to emphasize the value of effort.

6. Providing Supportive Relationships:

    Purpose: Build a network of supportive connections.

    Strategies: Encourage strong relationships with family, friends, teachers, and mentors.

    Tip: Create opportunities for your child to interact with supportive adults and peers.

7. Encouraging Healthy Risk-Taking:

    Purpose: Help children learn from new experiences and challenges.

    Strategies: Support your child in trying new activities and stepping out of their comfort zone.

    Tip: Celebrate successes and discuss what they learned from failures.

8. Promoting Physical Health:

    Purpose: Support overall well-being and stress management.

    Strategies: Encourage regular physical activity, healthy eating, and adequate sleep.

    Tip: Engage in family activities that promote physical health, such as hiking or playing sports together.

Real-Life Example

Consider the story of Lily, a nine-year-old girl who struggled with anxiety and low self-esteem. Her parents, Anna and Tom, decided to focus on building her resilience. They encouraged Lily to take on small responsibilities at home and supported her in trying new activities, such as joining a soccer team. They modeled resilience by sharing their own experiences of overcoming challenges and practicing problem-solving skills together. They also promoted emotional awareness by discussing feelings and teaching relaxation techniques. Over time, Lily became more confident, learned to manage her anxiety, and developed a stronger sense of self-worth. The focus on resilience significantly improved her emotional well-being and ability to handle challenges.

Reflection Questions

1. What challenges has your child faced, and how did they respond?

2. Which strategies can you implement to help build your child's resilience?

3. How can you model resilient behaviour and support your child in developing resilience?

Conclusion

Building resilience is essential for a child's emotional well-being and long-term success. By encouraging independence, modeling resilient behaviour, teaching problem-solving skills, promoting emotional awareness, fostering a growth mindset, providing supportive relationships, encouraging healthy risk-taking, and promoting physical health, parents and educators can help children develop the resilience they need to thrive. Embrace the journey of building resilience and watch as your child grows into a confident, capable, and emotionally resilient individual.

As we continue this journey through the book, we will explore more strategies and techniques to nurture your child's emotional development. Embrace the power of resilience, and watch as your child thrives in a supportive and nurturing environment.

❖❖

Nelson Mandela: "Do not judge me by my successes, judge me by how many times I fell down and got back up again."

[Nelson Mandela, former President of South Africa and an iconic figure in the struggle against apartheid, underscores the essence of resilience in the face of repeated setbacks. This quote resonates with the theme of building resilience, emphasizing perseverance and the ability to bounce back.]

Maya Angelou: "You may encounter many defeats, but you must not be defeated. In fact, it may be necessary to encounter the defeats, so you can know who you are, what you can rise from, how you can still come out of it."

[Maya Angelou, celebrated poet and civil rights activist, emphasizes the importance of overcoming adversity to build resilience. This quote aligns with the theme of building resilience by highlighting the growth that comes from facing and overcoming challenges.]

Chapter 17

Mindfulness and Emotional Regulation

Introduction

Mindfulness is a powerful tool that helps children develop emotional regulation, self-awareness, and resilience. By teaching mindfulness practices, parents and educators can support children in managing their emotions, reducing stress, and enhancing their overall well-being. In this chapter, we will explore the benefits of mindfulness, practical strategies for incorporating mindfulness into daily routines, and techniques for fostering emotional regulation.

The Benefits of Mindfulness

Mindfulness involves paying full attention to the present moment without judgment. It helps children develop the ability to observe their thoughts and feelings calmly and objectively. The benefits of mindfulness for children include:

1. Improved Emotional Regulation:

    Mindfulness helps children recognize and manage their emotions effectively.

    Example: A child who practices mindfulness can better handle frustration and anger without acting out.

2. Reduced Stress and Anxiety:

    Mindfulness techniques can reduce symptoms of stress and anxiety.

    Example: A child who practices deep breathing can calm themselves during a stressful situation.

3. Enhanced Focus and Concentration:

    Mindfulness improves attention span and cognitive function.

    Example: A child who engages in mindfulness exercises can concentrate better on schoolwork.

4. Increased Self-Awareness:

    Mindfulness fosters greater awareness of thoughts, feelings, and bodily sensations.

    Example: A child who practices mindfulness becomes more attuned to their emotional state and needs.

5. Better Relationships:

    Mindfulness promotes empathy, compassion, and effective communication.

    Example: A child who practices mindfulness can respond more thoughtfully in social interactions.

Practical Strategies for Incorporating Mindfulness

1. Mindful Breathing:

    Purpose: Teach children to focus on their breath to calm their mind and body.

    Technique: Guide your child to take slow, deep breaths, paying attention to the sensation of air entering and leaving their body.

    Tip: Use a visual aid, such as a pinwheel or a feather, to make the exercise engaging for younger children.

2. Body Scan:

    Purpose: Help children develop body awareness and release tension.

Technique: Guide your child to mentally scan their body from head to toe, noticing any areas of tension, and consciously relaxing them.

Tip: Use a soothing voice and gentle background music to create a calming atmosphere.

3. Mindful Listening:

Purpose: Enhance focus and awareness through attentive listening.

Technique: Have your child sit quietly and listen to the surrounding sounds, focusing on each sound without judgment.

Tip: Use nature sounds, such as birds chirping or water flowing, to create a peaceful environment.

4. Mindful Eating:

Purpose: Encourage children to savor their food and develop gratitude for their meals.

Technique: Guide your child to eat slowly, paying attention to the taste, texture, and smell of their food.

Tip: Practice mindful eating together as a family to reinforce the habit.

5. Gratitude Practice:

Purpose: Foster a positive mindset and appreciation for the present moment.

Technique: Encourage your child to write down or share three things they are grateful for each day.

Tip: Create a gratitude jar where family members can add notes of gratitude and read them together periodically.

6. Mindful Movement:

    Purpose: Combine physical activity with mindfulness to enhance body awareness and relaxation.

    Technique: Guide your child through gentle movements, such as yoga or tai chi, focusing on the sensations and breath.

    Tip: Use online resources or classes to learn mindful movement techniques together.

7. Guided Imagery:

    Purpose: Help children use their imagination to create a sense of calm and relaxation.

    Technique: Lead your child through a visualization exercise, such as imagining a peaceful place or a calming scene.

    Tip: Use guided imagery scripts or recordings to provide structure and guidance.

Techniques for Fostering Emotional Regulation

1. Emotion Identification:

    Purpose: Help children recognize and label their emotions.

Technique: Use an emotion wheel or feelings chart to discuss different emotions and their triggers.

Tip: Encourage your child to express their feelings verbally or through creative activities, such as drawing or writing.

2. Coping Skills Toolbox:

Purpose: Provide children with a variety of strategies to manage their emotions.

Technique: Create a toolbox filled with items and activities that help your child cope with stress, such as stress balls, coloring books, or calming music.

Tip: Teach your child to choose an appropriate coping skill from the toolbox when they feel overwhelmed.

3. Positive Self-Talk:

Purpose: Encourage children to use affirming and supportive language with themselves.

Technique: Teach your child to replace negative thoughts with positive statements, such as "I can do this" or "I am capable."

Tip: Model positive self-talk in your own behaviour and praise your child for using it.

4. Problem-Solving Skills:

Purpose: Equip children with the ability to address challenges effectively.

Technique: Guide your child through a problem-solving process, including identifying the problem, brainstorming solutions, and evaluating outcomes.

Tip: Use real-life situations to practice problem-solving together.

5. Relaxation Techniques:

Purpose: Help children calm their mind and body during stressful situations.

Technique: Teach relaxation techniques such as progressive muscle relaxation, deep breathing, or using a calming object.

Tip: Practice these techniques regularly so your child becomes comfortable using them independently.

Real-Life Example

Consider the story of Max, an eight-year-old boy who often felt anxious and had difficulty managing his emotions. His parents, Jane and Tom, decided to introduce mindfulness practices into his daily routine. They started with simple breathing exercises and gradually incorporated body scans, mindful listening, and gratitude practices. They also created a coping skills toolbox filled with items that helped Max calm down when he felt overwhelmed. Over time, Max became more adept at recognizing his emotions and using mindfulness techniques to manage them. The consistent practice of mindfulness significantly improved Max's emotional regulation and overall well-being.

Reflection Questions

1. How can you incorporate mindfulness practices into your child's daily routine?

2. What techniques can help your child improve their emotional regulation?

3. How can you model mindfulness and emotional regulation for your child?

Conclusion

Mindfulness is a powerful tool for fostering emotional regulation and overall well-being in children. By incorporating mindfulness practices such as mindful breathing, body scans, and gratitude exercises, parents and educators can help children develop self-awareness, reduce stress, and enhance their emotional resilience. Embrace the practice of mindfulness and watch as your child grows into a calm, focused, and emotionally balanced individual.

As we continue this journey through the book, we will explore more strategies and techniques to nurture your child's emotional development. Embrace the power of mindfulness and emotional regulation, and watch as your child thrives in a supportive and nurturing environment.

***

Jon Kabat-Zinn: "You can't stop the waves, but you can learn to surf."

[Jon Kabat-Zinn, the founder of Mindfulness-Based Stress Reduction (MBSR), emphasizes the power of mindfulness in

managing life's challenges. This quote resonates with the theme of mindfulness and emotional regulation by highlighting the ability to navigate difficulties with mindfulness practices.]

Thich Nhat Hanh: "Feelings come and go like clouds in a windy sky. Conscious breathing is my anchor."

[Thich Nhat Hanh, a renowned Buddhist monk and mindfulness teacher, underscores the importance of mindful breathing in maintaining emotional stability. This quote aligns with the theme of mindfulness and emotional regulation, illustrating how mindfulness can help manage and stabilize emotions.]

Chapter 18

Parent-Teacher Collaboration

Introduction

Parent-teacher collaboration is crucial for a child's academic success and emotional well-being. When parents and teachers work together, they create a supportive and cohesive environment that fosters a child's growth. Effective communication and cooperation between home and school can address challenges, celebrate achievements, and ensure that each child's unique needs are met.

In this chapter, we will explore the importance of parent-teacher collaboration, strategies for building strong partnerships, and practical tips for maintaining effective communication. By understanding and implementing these strategies, parents and educators can work together to support children's holistic development.

The Importance of Parent-Teacher Collaboration

Parent-teacher collaboration offers numerous benefits, including:

1. Enhanced Academic Performance:

    Children perform better academically when parents and teachers collaborate and share insights.

    Example: Regular communication about a child's progress and needs leads to tailored support and interventions.

2. Improved Emotional Well-Being:

    A unified approach between home and school fosters a sense of security and consistency for children.

    Example: Consistent reinforcement of positive behaviours at home and school helps children feel supported and understood.

3. Early Identification of Issues:

    Collaboration enables early detection and intervention for academic or emotional challenges.

    Example: Teachers and parents working together can quickly identify and address issues such as learning disabilities or behavioural problems.

4. Stronger Support Network:

    A collaborative relationship provides a robust support system for children, enhancing their resilience and confidence.

    Example: Children feel more confident knowing that their parents and teachers are united in their efforts to support them.

5. Positive Relationships:

    Strong parent-teacher relationships set a positive example for children, teaching them the value of teamwork and communication.

    Example: Seeing parents and teachers interact respectfully and cooperatively models healthy relationship skills for children.

Strategies for Building Strong Parent-Teacher Partnerships

1. Open Communication:

    Purpose: Foster trust and transparency between parents and teachers.

Strategies: Establish regular communication channels, such as emails, phone calls, or parent-teacher conferences.

Tip: Share updates on a child's progress, achievements, and any concerns promptly.

2. Setting Common Goals:

    Purpose: Align efforts to support the child's development.

    Strategies: Collaborate to set academic and behavioural goals for the child.

    Tip: Revisit and adjust goals as needed based on the child's progress and changing needs.

3. Active Participation:

    Purpose: Encourage parents to be involved in their child's education.

    Strategies: Invite parents to participate in school events, volunteer opportunities, and classroom activities.

    Tip: Provide flexible options for involvement to accommodate different schedules and availability.

4. Regular Feedback:

    Purpose: Keep parents informed about their child's progress and areas for improvement.

    Strategies: Use report cards, progress reports, and informal updates to provide regular feedback.

Tip: Highlight both strengths and areas for growth to give a balanced perspective.

5. Collaborative Problem-Solving:

Purpose: Address challenges and find solutions together.

Strategies: Hold meetings to discuss concerns and brainstorm strategies collaboratively.

Tip: Focus on the child's needs and maintain a positive, solution-oriented approach.

6. Cultural Sensitivity:

Purpose: Respect and acknowledge diverse backgrounds and perspectives.

Strategies: Be aware of cultural differences and incorporate culturally relevant practices into communication and activities.

Tip: Seek input from parents about their cultural practices and preferences.

Practical Tips for Maintaining Effective Communication

1. Scheduled Meetings:

Purpose: Ensure regular and consistent communication.

Strategies: Schedule parent-teacher conferences at the beginning of the school year and follow up with periodic meetings.

Tip: Use these meetings to review the child's progress, discuss goals, and address any concerns.

2. Daily or Weekly Updates:

    Purpose: Keep parents informed about daily or weekly activities and progress.

    Strategies: Use communication tools, such as newsletters, emails, or school apps, to provide updates.

    Tip: Include positive news and upcoming events to keep parents engaged and informed.

3. Two-Way Communication:

    Purpose: Encourage active dialogue between parents and teachers.

    Strategies: Provide opportunities for parents to share their observations, concerns, and suggestions.

    Tip: Create a welcoming atmosphere where parents feel comfortable voicing their thoughts.

4. Use of Technology:

    Purpose: Facilitate convenient and efficient communication.

    Strategies: Utilize technology, such as email, school websites, and communication apps, to stay connected.

    Tip: Ensure that all parents have access to and are comfortable using these tools.

5. Positive Reinforcement:

    Purpose: Build a positive and supportive relationship.

    Strategies: Share positive feedback and celebrate the child's achievements regularly.

    Tip: Highlight specific examples of the child's strengths and successes.

6. Consistency:

    Purpose: Provide a stable and predictable communication routine.

    Strategies: Maintain a consistent schedule for updates and meetings.

    Tip: Set reminders for regular communication to ensure it remains a priority.

Real-Life Example

Consider the story of Jake, a seven-year-old boy who was struggling academically and socially. His parents, Lisa and John, and his teacher, Mrs. Patel, decided to work together to support Jake's development. They scheduled regular meetings to discuss Jake's progress and challenges, set common goals for his academic and social growth, and maintained open communication through weekly emails. Lisa and John participated in school events and volunteered in the classroom, strengthening their connection with Mrs. Patel and the school community. This collaborative approach helped identify Jake's learning needs early, leading to tailored interventions and support. Over time, Jake's academic performance improved, and he became more confident and socially engaged. The strong partnership between his parents and teacher played a crucial role in his success.

Reflection Questions

1. How can you improve communication and collaboration with your child's teacher?

2. What strategies can you implement to support your child's development at home and school?

3. How can you create a positive and cooperative relationship with your child's educators?

Conclusion

Parent-teacher collaboration is essential for a child's academic success and emotional well-being. By fostering open communication, setting common goals, actively participating, providing regular feedback, solving problems collaboratively, and respecting cultural differences, parents and educators can work together to support children's holistic development. Embrace the power of partnership and watch as your child thrives in a supportive and cohesive environment.

As we continue this journey through the book, we will explore more strategies and techniques to nurture your child's emotional development. Embrace the collaborative role of parents and teachers, and watch as your child grows into a confident, capable, and emotionally resilient individual.

———◆◆———

Henry Ford: "Coming together is a beginning, staying together is progress, and working together is success."

[Henry Ford, the founder of the Ford Motor Company and pioneer of modern assembly lines, emphasizes the importance of collaboration and teamwork. This quote aligns with the theme of parent-teacher collaboration by highlighting the value of sustained cooperative efforts in achieving success.]

Helen Keller: "Alone we can do so little; together we can do so much."

[Helen Keller, an author, activist, and lecturer who overcame the challenges of being both deaf and blind, underscores the power of working together. This quote resonates with the theme of parent-teacher collaboration, emphasizing how much more can be achieved when parents and teachers join forces to support children's development.]

Chapter 19

Sibling Relationships and Emotional Development

Introduction

Sibling relationships play a crucial role in a child's emotional development. These relationships are often the longest-lasting connections in a person's life and significantly influence their social skills, emotional regulation, and self-esteem. Understanding and nurturing positive sibling relationships can help children develop the emotional resilience and interpersonal skills they need to thrive.

In this chapter, we will explore the impact of sibling relationships on emotional development, common challenges, and practical strategies for fostering healthy and supportive sibling interactions. By addressing these aspects, parents and educators can create an environment where sibling bonds flourish and contribute positively to each child's growth.

The Impact of Sibling Relationships on Emotional Development

Sibling relationships can shape various aspects of emotional development:

1. Social Skills:

   Sibling interactions provide opportunities for practicing communication, negotiation, and conflict resolution.

   Example: Siblings learn to share, take turns, and understand different perspectives through their daily interactions.

2. Emotional Regulation:

   Siblings help each other learn to manage emotions, offering support and guidance during difficult times.

   Example: An older sibling comforting a younger sibling during a stressful situation helps both develop empathy and emotional control.

3. Self-Esteem:

   Positive sibling relationships can boost self-esteem and provide a sense of belonging and security.

   Example: A sibling who receives praise and encouragement from their brother or sister feels more confident and valued.

4. Conflict Resolution:

   Sibling conflicts offer a natural context for learning how to resolve disagreements constructively.

   Example: Siblings who argue over toys and then find a way to share develop important problem-solving skills.

5. Role Modeling:

   Older siblings often serve as role models, influencing the behaviours and attitudes of younger siblings.

   Example: A younger sibling may emulate the positive study habits or social skills of an older sibling.

Common Challenges in Sibling Relationships

While sibling relationships can be a source of support and growth, they also come with challenges:

1. Sibling Rivalry:

   Competition for parental attention and resources can lead to jealousy and conflicts.

Example: Siblings who constantly compare themselves to each other may feel resentful and competitive.

2. Differing Personalities:

   Variations in temperament and interests can cause misunderstandings and disagreements.

   Example: An introverted child may struggle to relate to an extroverted sibling who seeks constant interaction.

3. Age Differences:

   Significant age gaps can create challenges in finding common interests and activities.

   Example: A teenager may find it difficult to connect with a much younger sibling who is still in early childhood.

4. Parental Favoritism:

   Perceived favoritism can damage sibling relationships and individual self-esteem.

   Example: A child who feels that a sibling is favored may develop feelings of inadequacy and resentment.

5. External Stressors:

   Family stressors such as financial difficulties, parental conflict, or major life changes can exacerbate sibling tensions.

Example: Siblings may take out their frustrations on each other during times of family stress.

Practical Strategies for Fostering Healthy Sibling Relationships

1. Encouraging Positive Interactions:

    Purpose: Promote bonding and positive experiences between siblings.

    Activities: Plan shared activities that both siblings enjoy, such as games, crafts, or outdoor adventures.

    Tip: Highlight and praise instances of cooperation and kindness between siblings.

2. Teaching Conflict Resolution:

    Purpose: Equip siblings with the skills to handle disagreements constructively.

    Techniques: Teach active listening, empathy, and problem-solving skills.

    Tip: Model and role-play conflict resolution scenarios to provide practical examples.

3. Setting Clear Expectations:

    Purpose: Establish guidelines for respectful behaviour and fair treatment.

    Strategies: Create family rules that emphasize respect, sharing, and taking turns.

Tip: Consistently enforce rules and address conflicts calmly and fairly.

4. Avoiding Comparisons:

Purpose: Foster individual self-esteem and reduce competition.

Strategies: Focus on each child's unique strengths and accomplishments.

Tip: Use specific praise that acknowledges individual efforts and qualities.

5. Spending One-on-One Time:

Purpose: Ensure each child feels valued and receives individual attention.

Strategies: Schedule regular one-on-one activities with each child.

Tip: Use this time to strengthen your relationship with each child and address their specific needs.

6. Creating a Supportive Environment:

Purpose: Provide a safe space for siblings to express their feelings and resolve issues.

Strategies: Encourage open communication and validate each child's emotions.

Tip: Hold family meetings to discuss concerns and celebrate successes together.

7. Encouraging Cooperative Tasks:

    Purpose: Promote teamwork and shared responsibility.

    Activities: Assign chores or projects that require siblings to work together.

    Tip: Rotate tasks to ensure fairness and encourage collaboration.

Real-Life Example

Consider the story of Mia and Alex, siblings with a three-year age gap. Mia, the older sister, often felt overshadowed by her younger brother's outgoing personality. Their parents, Sarah and David, noticed the growing tension and decided to intervene. They scheduled regular family activities that both children enjoyed, such as hiking and board games. They also established clear rules for resolving conflicts and encouraged Mia and Alex to talk about their feelings openly. Additionally, Sarah and David made an effort to spend one-on-one time with each child, recognizing and celebrating their individual strengths. Over time, Mia and Alex developed a stronger bond, learning to appreciate each other's differences and work together harmoniously.

Reflection Questions

1. How do your children's personalities and interests influence their interactions?

2. What strategies can you implement to reduce sibling rivalry and promote positive relationships?

3. How can you create opportunities for your children to bond and resolve conflicts constructively?

Conclusion

Sibling relationships are a vital component of a child's emotional development. By understanding the impact of these relationships and addressing common challenges, parents and educators can foster healthy, supportive interactions between siblings. Encouraging positive interactions, teaching conflict resolution, setting clear expectations, avoiding comparisons, spending one-on-one time, creating a supportive environment, and promoting cooperative tasks are effective strategies for nurturing strong sibling bonds.

As we continue this journey through the book, we will explore more strategies and techniques to nurture your child's emotional development. Embrace the importance of sibling relationships and watch as your children grow into emotionally resilient and socially skilled individuals.

———◆◆———

Clara Ortega: "To the outside world, we all grow old. But not to brothers and sisters. We know each other as we always were. We know each other's hearts. We share private family jokes. We remember family feuds and secrets, family griefs and joys."

[Clara Ortega, author and educator, highlights the unique and enduring nature of sibling relationships. This quote resonates with the theme of sibling relationships and emotional development by

emphasizing the deep emotional bonds and shared experiences that siblings have.]

Jane Mersky Leder: "Sibling relationships... outlast marriages, survive the death of parents, resurface after quarrels that would sink any friendship. They flourish in a thousand incarnations of closeness and distance, warmth, loyalty, and distrust."

[Jane Mersky Leder, journalist and author, captures the complex and enduring nature of sibling relationships. This quote aligns with the theme of sibling relationships and emotional development, showcasing how these bonds persist through various stages and challenges in life.]

Chapter 20

Parental Self-Care

Introduction

Parental self-care is essential for fostering a healthy family environment and supporting a child's emotional development. When parents prioritize their well-being, they are better equipped to handle the challenges of parenting and provide the emotional support their children need. In this chapter, we will explore the importance of parental self-care, common obstacles, and practical strategies to incorporate self-care into daily routines. By nurturing themselves, parents can create a more balanced and nurturing environment for their children.

The Importance of Parental Self-C care

Parental self-care is crucial for several reasons:

1. Emotional Well-Being:

    Parents who take care of their emotional health are more patient, empathetic, and resilient.

    Example: A parent who practices self-care can handle a child's tantrum with calmness and understanding.

2. Role Modeling:

    Demonstrating self-care teaches children the importance of looking after their own well-being.

    Example: A parent who makes time for exercise and relaxation shows their child how to maintain a healthy lifestyle.

3. Stress Reduction:

    Self-care practices help reduce stress, preventing burnout and promoting overall health.

    Example: A parent who engages in regular relaxation techniques can manage the demands of parenting more effectively.

4. Improved Relationships:

   Parents who take care of themselves have more energy and emotional capacity to build strong relationships with their children.

   Example: A parent who is well-rested and relaxed can engage more meaningfully with their child's activities and needs.

5. Balanced Life:

   Prioritizing self-care helps parents maintain a healthy balance between personal, professional, and family life.

   Example: A parent who sets boundaries and allocates time for self-care is more likely to feel fulfilled and less overwhelmed.

Common Obstacles to Parental Self-Care

Many parents face obstacles that make self-care challenging:

1. Guilt:

   Parents often feel guilty for taking time for themselves, believing they should always prioritize their children.

   Example: A parent who feels guilty for going out with friends because they think they should be home with their child.

2. Lack of Time:

    Busy schedules and numerous responsibilities can make finding time for self-care difficult.

    Example: A parent who struggles to find time for exercise due to work and childcare commitments.

3. Financial Constraints:

    Limited financial resources can restrict access to certain self-care activities.

    Example: A parent who cannot afford a gym membership or a spa day.

4. Perceived Selfishness:

    Some parents believe that focusing on their own needs is selfish.

    Example: A parent who avoids taking breaks because they think it's selfish to rest when there are chores to be done.

5. Lack of Support:

    Without a support network, parents may find it hard to prioritize their well-being.

    Example: A single parent who has no one to help with childcare, making it challenging to take personal time.

Practical Strategies for Incorporating Self-Care

1. Setting Boundaries:

    Purpose: Protect personal time and prevent burnout.

    Strategies: Establish clear boundaries between work, family, and personal time.

    Tip: Communicate your needs to family members and ask for their support in respecting your boundaries.

2. Creating a Self-Care Routine:

    Purpose: Ensure regular self-care practices.

    Strategies: Schedule self-care activities as part of your daily or weekly routine.

    Tip: Start with small, manageable activities and gradually increase the time dedicated to self-care.

3. Practicing Mindfulness:

    Purpose: Enhance emotional regulation and reduce stress.

    Activities: Engage in mindfulness practices such as meditation, deep breathing, or yoga.

    Tip: Incorporate mindfulness into everyday activities, such as mindful eating or mindful walking.

4. Prioritizing Physical Health:

    Purpose: Improve overall well-being and energy levels.

Activities: Engage in regular exercise, maintain a balanced diet, and ensure adequate sleep.

Tip: Find physical activities you enjoy and incorporate them into your routine, such as dancing, swimming, or hiking.

5. Seeking Social Support:

Purpose: Build a supportive network for emotional and practical assistance.

Strategies: Connect with friends, join parenting groups, or seek support from family members.

Tip: Make time for social activities that recharge you, such as coffee with a friend or a group outing.

6. Engaging in Hobbies:

Purpose: Foster personal fulfillment and relaxation.

Activities: Pursue hobbies and interests that bring you joy, such as reading, gardening, or crafting.

Tip: Dedicate regular time to your hobbies and treat them as essential parts of your routine.

7. Asking for Help:

Purpose: Share responsibilities and reduce stress.

Strategies: Delegate tasks and seek help from your partner, family, or friends when needed.

Tip: Be specific about what you need and accept offers of help graciously.

8. Practicing Gratitude:

   Purpose: Foster a positive mindset and emotional resilience.

   Activities: Keep a gratitude journal, reflect on positive experiences, and express gratitude to others.

   Tip: Incorporate gratitude practices into your daily routine, such as sharing three things you're grateful for each day.

Real-Life Example

Consider the story of Emily, a mother of two who struggled to find time for herself amidst her busy schedule. She often felt overwhelmed and guilty for wanting a break. After recognizing the importance of self-care, Emily decided to make some changes. She set clear boundaries for work and family time, communicated her needs to her partner, and scheduled regular self-care activities, such as morning yoga and weekend walks. Emily also joined a local parenting group, which provided both social support and practical advice. These changes helped Emily feel more balanced and energized, allowing her to be more present and patient with her children. The focus on self-care significantly improved her emotional well-being and overall family dynamics.

Reflection Questions

1. What are your current obstacles to practicing self-care?

2. How can you incorporate self-care into your daily or weekly routine?

3. Who can you turn to for support in prioritizing your well-being?

Conclusion

Parental self-care is vital for fostering a healthy family environment and supporting a child's emotional development. By setting boundaries, creating a self-care routine, practicing mindfulness, prioritizing physical health, seeking social support, engaging in hobbies, asking for help, and practicing gratitude, parents can nurture their well-being and enhance their ability to care for their children. Embrace the importance of self-care and watch as your family thrives in a balanced and nurturing environment.

As we continue this journey through the book, we will explore more strategies and techniques to nurture your child's emotional development. Embrace the power of self-care and watch as your own well-being positively impacts your child's growth and happiness.

———✦✦———

Eleanor Brown: "Self-care is not about self-indulgence, it's about self-preservation."

[Eleanor Brown, author and speaker, emphasizes the importance of self-care as a means of maintaining one's well-being. This quote aligns with the theme of parental self-care by reinforcing that taking care of oneself is crucial for long-term health and resilience.]

Parker Palmer: "Self-care is never a selfish act—it is simply good stewardship of the only gift I have, the gift I was put on earth to offer others."

[Parker Palmer, educator and author, highlights the significance of self-care as a way to maintain one's ability to contribute meaningfully to others. This quote resonates with the theme of parental self-care, underscoring that by caring for oneself, parents can better fulfill their roles and responsibilities.]

Additional Chapter

Trauma-Informed Parenting

Introduction

Trauma can significantly impact a child's emotional and behavioral development. Understanding the effects of trauma and implementing trauma-informed parenting strategies can help create a safe and supportive environment for children who have experienced trauma. This chapter explores the nature of trauma, its impact on children, and practical approaches to trauma-informed parenting.

Understanding Trauma

Definition and Types of Trauma:

Acute Trauma: Results from a single distressing event (e.g., natural disasters, accidents).

Chronic Trauma: Involves repeated and prolonged exposure to distressing events (e.g., abuse, neglect).

Complex Trauma: Arises from exposure to multiple traumatic events, often within a caregiving relationship.

Impact of Trauma on Children:

Emotional Effects: Anxiety, depression, anger, and fear.

Behavioral Effects: Aggression, withdrawal, hyperactivity, and difficulties with concentration.

Cognitive Effects: Impaired learning, memory issues, and difficulty in problem-solving.

Physical Effects: Sleep disturbances, somatic complaints (e.g., headaches, stomachaches), and developmental delays.

Trauma-Informed Parenting Strategies

Creating a Safe Environment:

Physical Safety: Ensure the child's environment is secure and free from threats.

Emotional Safety: Build trust through consistent, nurturing interactions.

Predictability: Maintain routines and provide clear expectations to reduce anxiety.

Building Emotional Resilience:

Validation: Acknowledge the child's feelings and experiences without judgment.

Empathy: Show understanding and compassion for the child's emotional state.

Support: Provide reassurance and be present for the child during difficult times.

Practical Techniques:

Grounding Techniques: Help children stay present and manage anxiety (e.g., deep breathing, sensory activities).

Therapeutic Play: Use play as a means for children to express and process their emotions.

Positive Reinforcement: Encourage and reward positive behaviors to build self-esteem and confidence.

Professional Support:

Therapy: Engage with child psychologists or trauma specialists for professional guidance.

Support Groups: Participate in groups with other parents and caregivers of traumatized children to share experiences and strategies.

School Collaboration: Work with educators to ensure the child receives appropriate support in their academic environment.

Real-Life Example

Consider the case of Emily, a six-year-old girl who experienced chronic trauma due to domestic violence. Emily's mother, Sarah, noticed her daughter's increased anxiety, frequent nightmares, and reluctance to engage with peers. Sarah sought the help of a trauma specialist, who recommended creating a safe and predictable home environment, validating Emily's feelings, and using grounding techniques during episodes of anxiety.

Sarah also collaborated with Emily's teachers to ensure they were aware of her trauma history and provided consistent support at school. Over time, with professional therapy and a nurturing home environment, Emily's anxiety reduced, and she began to thrive both emotionally and academically.

Reflection Questions

1. How can you create a safe and supportive environment for a child who has experienced trauma?

2. Which trauma-informed strategies can you implement to support your child's emotional and behavioral development?

3. How can you collaborate with professionals to provide comprehensive support for a traumatized child?

Conclusion

Trauma-informed parenting requires understanding the profound impact trauma can have on a child and implementing strategies that provide safety, support, and validation. By adopting trauma-informed practices, parents and caregivers can help children heal and build resilience, leading to healthier emotional and behavioral development.

Social Justice and Empathy in Childhood

Introduction

Teaching children about empathy, fairness, and social justice is crucial for their emotional and social development. This chapter explores the importance of these values, practical ways to incorporate them into daily life, and strategies to nurture compassionate and responsible individuals.

Understanding Social Justice and Empathy

Defining Empathy:

Cognitive Empathy: Understanding others' perspectives and feelings.

Emotional Empathy: Feeling what others feel and sharing in their emotional experiences.

Compassionate Empathy: Taking action to help others based on understanding and sharing their feelings.

Defining Social Justice:

Fairness: Ensuring everyone has equal opportunities and rights.

Equity: Recognizing and addressing systemic inequalities and providing support based on individual needs.

Inclusion: Embracing diversity and ensuring all voices are heard and valued.

Practical Strategies for Teaching Empathy and Social Justice

Modeling Behavior:

Demonstrate Empathy: Show empathy in your interactions with others and discuss your feelings and actions with your child.

Promote Fairness: Treat others fairly and discuss the importance of fairness in daily situations.

Encouraging Compassionate Actions:

Volunteer Together: Participate in community service projects as a family.

Discuss Current Events: Talk about social justice issues in age-appropriate ways and encourage your child to ask questions and express their thoughts.

Using Literature and Media:

Books and Stories: Read books that highlight empathy, diversity, and social justice themes.

Movies and Shows: Watch and discuss media that portray characters demonstrating empathy and standing up for justice.

Creating Opportunities for Empathy:

Role-Playing: Engage in role-playing activities that encourage children to see situations from others' perspectives.

Empathy Games: Use games and activities designed to build empathy and understanding.

Real-Life Example

Consider the story of Ben, a ten-year-old boy who struggled with understanding his classmates' different backgrounds. His parents, Tom and Lisa, began volunteering at a local food bank and included Ben in their activities. They also read books about diverse cultures and discussed current events related to social justice at the dinner table.

Through these experiences, Ben developed a greater sense of empathy and fairness. He started showing more compassion towards his peers and became actively involved in school initiatives promoting inclusion and equity.

Reflection Questions

1. How can you model empathy and fairness in your daily interactions?

2. What activities can you incorporate to teach your child about social justice?

3. How can you use literature and media to discuss these values with your child?

Conclusion

Fostering empathy and social justice in children is essential for their emotional and social growth. By modeling these values, encouraging compassionate actions, and using literature and media, parents and educators can nurture children who are not only emotionally intelligent but also committed to making the world a fairer and more inclusive place.

Additional Chapter

The Role of Emotional Literacy

Introduction

Emotional literacy, the ability to recognize, understand, and manage emotions, is a crucial aspect of a child's development. Teaching emotional literacy equips children with the skills needed to navigate their emotional landscape, fostering better communication, empathy, and resilience. This chapter explores the importance of emotional literacy, practical activities for teaching these skills, and strategies to integrate emotional literacy into daily life.

Understanding Emotional Literacy

Defining Emotional Literacy:

Recognition: The ability to identify and label emotions in oneself and others.

Understanding: Comprehending the causes and consequences of emotions.

Management: Developing strategies to express and regulate emotions appropriately.

Components of Emotional Literacy:

Self-Awareness: Understanding one's own emotions.

Self-Regulation: Managing emotions in a healthy way.

Social Awareness: Recognizing and understanding others' emotions.

Relationship Skills: Building healthy relationships through effective communication and empathy.

Responsible Decision-Making: Making choices based on ethical standards, safety, and social norms.

Importance of Emotional Literacy

Enhanced Communication: Children who are emotionally literate can express their feelings clearly and effectively, reducing misunderstandings and conflicts.

Improved Emotional Regulation: Emotional literacy helps children manage their emotions, reducing the likelihood of emotional outbursts and promoting resilience.

Increased Empathy: Understanding and recognizing emotions in others fosters empathy and strengthens social bonds.

Better Academic Performance:

Emotionally literate children tend to perform better academically, as they are more focused, less stressed, and better able to cope with challenges.

Stronger Relationships:

Emotional literacy skills contribute to healthier relationships with peers, teachers, and family members.

Practical Activities for Teaching Emotional Literacy

Emotion Cards:

Description: Use cards depicting different emotions to help children identify and label their feelings.

Activity: Have children pick a card that represents how they feel and explain why they chose it.

Feelings Journal:

Description: Encourage children to keep a journal where they can write or draw about their daily emotions.

Activity: Reflect on journal entries together, discussing the causes and responses to different emotions.

Storytelling:

Description: Use stories to discuss characters' emotions and motivations.

Activity: After reading a story, ask children how the characters felt and why, and how they would feel in a similar situation.

Role-Playing:

Description: Engage children in role-playing activities to practice expressing and managing emotions.

Activity: Create scenarios where children can act out different emotions and discuss appropriate responses.

Emotion Charades:

Description: Play a game where children act out emotions without speaking, and others guess the emotion.

Activity: Use this game to help children recognize non-verbal cues and express emotions physically.

Mindfulness Exercises:

Description: Incorporate mindfulness practices to help children become more aware of their emotions.

Activity: Practice deep breathing, guided imagery, or body scans to promote emotional awareness and regulation.

Integrating Emotional Literacy into Daily Life

Modeling Emotional Literacy:

Practice What You Preach: Demonstrate emotional literacy by expressing your own emotions clearly and managing them effectively.

Discuss Emotions: Talk about your feelings and why you feel that way, providing a model for children to emulate.

Creating an Emotionally Supportive Environment:

Safe Space: Create an environment where children feel safe to express their emotions without fear of judgment.

Active Listening: Listen attentively to children's emotions and validate their feelings.

Encouraging Emotional Expression:

Open Dialogue: Encourage regular discussions about emotions and experiences.

Validation: Acknowledge and validate children's emotions, showing empathy and understanding.

Using Everyday Opportunities:

Teachable Moments: Use daily interactions and experiences as opportunities to teach emotional literacy.

Reinforcement: Reinforce emotional literacy skills through praise and encouragement when children express and manage their emotions well.

Real-Life Example

Consider the case of Alex, an eight-year-old boy who struggled with expressing his emotions, often leading to frustration and anger. His parents, Maria and David, introduced emotional literacy activities at home. They used emotion cards to help Alex identify his feelings and kept a feelings journal where he could draw his emotions.

Maria and David also practiced mindfulness exercises with Alex to help him manage his anger. They modeled emotional literacy by expressing their own feelings and discussing them openly. Over time, Alex became more adept at recognizing and managing his emotions, resulting in fewer outbursts and improved relationships with his peers.

Reflection Questions

1. How can you integrate emotional literacy activities into your daily routine?

2. Which emotional literacy strategies can you implement to support your child's development?

3. How can you model emotional literacy in your interactions with your child?

Conclusion

Emotional literacy is a vital skill that underpins children's emotional and social development. By teaching children to recognize, understand, and manage their emotions, parents and educators can help them navigate the complexities of their emotional world. Through practical activities and everyday interactions, you can foster emotional literacy, contributing to your child's overall well-being and success.

Epilogue

As we come to the end of "Emotional Edge in Parenting: Your Complete Guide to Childhood Education," it is clear that nurturing a child's emotional development is a multifaceted journey. This journey is filled with moments of joy, challenges, growth, and learning for both the child and the parents. The insights, strategies, and examples provided throughout this book are designed to empower you to create a supportive and nurturing environment where your child can thrive emotionally, socially, and academically.

The importance of emotional development cannot be overstated. It is the foundation upon which all other aspects of growth are built. By prioritizing emotional well-being, we equip our children with the skills they need to navigate life's challenges, build strong relationships, and achieve their full potential.

Throughout this book, we have explored a wide range of topics, each contributing to the holistic development of your child:

1. Understanding Emotional Bonds: The crucial role of attachment and how it shapes a child's emotional foundation.

2. The Role of Play in Emotional Development: How play fosters emotional expression, social skills, and creativity.

3. Attachment Styles and Their Impact: The long-term effects of secure and insecure attachments on emotional development.

4. Social and Emotional Learning (SEL) Strategies: Practical techniques for integrating SEL into daily life.

5. Dealing with Common Childhood Challenges: Addressing anxiety, aggression, defiance, and withdrawal with empathy and effective strategies.

6. Cultural Influences on Emotional Development: Recognizing and respecting the impact of cultural backgrounds on a child's emotional growth.

7. Long-Term Benefits of Secure Attachments: How early bonds influence emotional regulation, resilience, and relationships.

8. Addressing Emotional and Behavioural Problems: Understanding and managing learning disabilities, ADD, and ADHD.

9. Practical Activities to Foster Emotional Growth: Engaging activities that promote emotional awareness, empathy, and social skills.

10. Inculcating Values and Providing Purpose: Teaching values and helping children find their purpose in life.

11. The Collaborative Role of Family: Strengthening family bonds and working together to support emotional development.

12. Balancing Physical Development and Emotional Well-Being: Integrating physical health and emotional resilience for holistic growth.

13. Understanding and Addressing Learning Disabilities: Supporting children with dyslexia, dysgraphia, dyscalculia, ADD, and ADHD.

14. Nurturing Gifted Children: Meeting the unique needs of gifted children and fostering their potential.

15. Technology and Emotional Development: Balancing technology use with activities that promote emotional well-being.

16. Building Resilience: Equipping children with the skills to handle adversity and bounce back from challenges.

17. Mindfulness and Emotional Regulation: Using mindfulness to enhance emotional awareness and self-regulation.

18. Parent-Teacher Collaboration: Working together to create a supportive and cohesive environment for children.

19. Sibling Relationships and Emotional Development: Fostering positive sibling interactions and addressing common challenges.

20. Parental Self-Care: The importance of self-care for parents and its impact on the family dynamic.

The journey of parenting and child education is ever-evolving. As you apply the strategies and insights from this book, remember that there is no one-size-fits-all approach. Every child is unique, and so are the circumstances and dynamics of each family. Be patient with yourself and your child, and embrace the learning process with an open heart and mind.

As you continue on this path, keep these key principles in mind:

Empathy: Understand and validate your child's emotions. Empathy strengthens your bond and helps your child feel seen and heard.

Consistency: Provide a stable and predictable environment. Consistency builds trust and security, which are essential for emotional development.

Communication: Maintain open and honest communication with your child, family members, and educators. Effective communication fosters understanding and collaboration.

Flexibility: Be willing to adapt and adjust your approaches as needed. Flexibility allows you to respond to your child's changing needs and circumstances.

Self-Care: Prioritize your own well-being. A balanced and healthy parent is better equipped to support and nurture their child's growth.

In conclusion, nurturing a child's emotional development is a profound and rewarding endeavor. By embracing the strategies and principles outlined in this book, you are taking important steps towards raising a resilient, empathetic, and emotionally intelligent individual. Your dedication and love are the most powerful tools on this journey. Trust in your abilities, continue to learn and grow, and remember that you are making a lasting impact on your child's life.

Thank you for embarking on this journey with "Emotional Edge in Parenting" May you find joy, fulfillment, and success as you nurture the emotional well-being of your child.

Acknowledgements

Writing "Emotional Edge in Parenting: Your Complete Guide to Childhood Education" has been a deeply fulfilling journey. This book is the result of collaboration, support, and inspiration from many individuals who have contributed their knowledge, experience, and encouragement along the way.

First and foremost, I want to express my heartfelt gratitude to the parents and educators who have trusted me with their experiences and challenges. Your stories, questions, and insights have been invaluable in shaping the content of this book. Your dedication to nurturing the emotional development of children is inspiring and has driven me to provide the most practical and empathetic guidance possible.

I would like to thank my family for their unwavering support and understanding throughout this process. To my wife, for her patience and encouragement, and to my child, whose curiosity and resilience continually remind me of the importance of emotional growth. Your love and belief in this project have been my greatest motivation.

A special thank you to my colleagues and mentors in the fields of psychology, education, and child development. Your expertise and feedback have enriched this book, ensuring that it is grounded in both research and practical application. Your contributions have been instrumental in making this guide comprehensive and accessible.

To the staff and students at the Golden Childhood Institution, thank you for being a source of inspiration and for allowing me to witness firsthand the impact of emotional education. Your enthusiasm for learning and growth fuels my passion for this work.

A sincere thank you to my editors and the publishing team for their meticulous work and dedication. Your efforts in refining and polishing this manuscript have been crucial to bringing this book to life.

Finally, to the readers of "Emotional Edge in Parenting," thank you for choosing to embark on this journey with me. Your commitment to enhancing the emotional well-being of children is commendable. I hope this book provides you with the tools, insights, and encouragement you need to make a positive difference in the lives of the children you nurture and educate.

With deepest gratitude,

Surajit Sarkar

About the Author

Surajit Sarkar is a distinguished educator, dedicated teacher, and passionate advocate for childhood education and emotional development. With over thirty years of exemplary service in the field of education, Surajit has touched the lives of countless children and their families, guiding them towards a brighter and more emotionally intelligent future.

Born and raised in West Bengal, India, Surajit's journey to education began in 1994. Two years later, in 1996, he founded the Golden Childhood Institution in Maynaguri, West Bengal, an esteemed school dedicated to fostering the holistic development of children. His institution has since become a beacon of innovative educational practices and emotional support for young minds.

Surajit's academic background in science, coupled with his deep interest in positive psychology, medical hypnosis, and Neuro-Linguistic Programming (NLP), has uniquely positioned him to address the complex emotional and psychological needs of children. He holds a Fellowship in Cardiac Rehabilitation from Apollo Hospital, Hyderabad, and is a member of several esteemed career counselling organizations in India and abroad, including the National Career Counselling Institute, the Counsellors

Council of India. He had been a member of the British Society of Experimental and Clinical Hypnosis, and the International Hypnosis Federation.

In addition to his extensive work with children, Surajit has authored two acclaimed books: "Nurturing Bonds: A Handbook for Emotional Development in Early Childhood" and "Parenting with Heart: Emotional Bonds for Early Childhood Development." His latest work, "Emotional Edge in Parenting: Your Complete Guide to Childhood Education," combines the wisdom and insights from his previous books with new, comprehensive strategies for nurturing emotionally intelligent children.

Surajit's dedication to childhood education and emotional development is not just professional, but deeply personal. He believes that emotions are the cornerstone of effective parenting and education, and his life's work is a testament to this belief. Through his writing, workshops, and ongoing advocacy, Surajit continues to inspire and empower parents, teachers, and caregivers to create nurturing, emotionally supportive environments for children worldwide.

When he's not working or writing, Surajit enjoys spending time with his family, engaging in community service, and exploring the natural beauty of West Bengal. His commitment to lifelong learning and his unwavering dedication to the well-being of children make him a revered figure in the field of childhood education.

Bibliography

The following sources have been instrumental in the research and development of " Emotional Edge in Parenting " These books, articles, and studies provide a solid foundation of knowledge and evidence-based practices that have informed the insights and strategies presented in this book. I am grateful to the authors and researchers whose work has contributed to the understanding of emotional development, parenting, and child education.

Books

1. Ainsworth, M. D. S., Blehar, M. C., Waters, E., & Wall, S. (1978). Patterns of Attachment: A Psychological Study of the Strange Situation. Lawrence Erlbaum Associates.

    This seminal work on attachment theory explores the different attachment styles and their impact on emotional development.

2. Baumrind, D. (1991). The Influence of Parenting Style on Adolescent Competence and Substance Use. Journal of Early Adolescence, 11(1), 56-95.

A comprehensive study on the effects of different parenting styles on children's development and behaviour.

3. Bronfenbrenner, U. (1979). The Ecology of Human Development: Experiments by Nature and Design. Harvard University Press.

Bronfenbrenner's ecological systems theory provides a framework for understanding the multiple influences on a child's development.

4. Dweck, C. S. (2006). Mindset: The New Psychology of Success. Random House.

Dweck's research on growth mindset emphasizes the importance of fostering resilience and a love for learning in children.

5. Goleman, D. (1995). Emotional Intelligence: Why It Can Matter More Than IQ. Bantam Books.

This influential book highlights the significance of emotional intelligence in personal and professional success.

6. Miller, A. (2002). The Drama of the Gifted Child: The Search for the True Self. Basic Books.

Miller's exploration of the emotional struggles of gifted children provides valuable insights for parents and educators.

7. Siegel, D. J., & Bryson, T. P. (2011). The Whole-Brain Child: 12 Revolutionary Strategies to Nurture Your Child's Developing Mind. Delacorte Press.

This book offers practical strategies for nurturing a child's emotional and cognitive development based on neuroscience.

8. Stern, D. N. (1985). The Interpersonal World of the Infant: A View from Psychoanalysis and Developmental Psychology. Basic Books.

Stern's work provides an in-depth look at early emotional development and the parent-infant relationship.

Articles and Journals

1. Bowlby, J. (1988). A Secure Base: Parent-Child Attachment and Healthy Human Development. Basic Books.

Bowlby's research on attachment theory underscores the importance of secure attachments in emotional development.

2. Brooks-Gunn, J., & Duncan, G. J. (1997). The Effects of Poverty on Children. The Future of Children, 7(2), 55-71.

This article examines the impact of socioeconomic factors on child development and well-being.

3. Deci, E. L., & Ryan, R. M. (2000). The "What" and "Why" of Goal Pursuits: Human Needs and the Self-

Determination of Behaviour. Psychological Inquiry, 11(4), 227-268.

An exploration of self-determination theory and its implications for motivation and emotional well-being.

4. Gardner, H. (1983). Frames of Mind: The Theory of Multiple Intelligences. Basic Books.

   Gardner's theory of multiple intelligences expands the understanding of human capabilities and learning styles.

5. Kabat-Zinn, J. (1994). Wherever You Go, There You Are: Mindfulness Meditation in Everyday Life. Hyperion.

   A foundational text on mindfulness practices and their benefits for emotional regulation and stress reduction.

6. Raver, C. C. (2004). Placing Emotional Self-Regulation in Sociocultural and Socioeconomic Contexts. Child Development, 75(2), 346-353.

   This article explores the influences of sociocultural and socioeconomic factors on children's emotional self-regulation.

7. Shonkoff, J. P., & Phillips, D. A. (Eds.). (2000). From Neurons to Neighborhoods: The Science of Early Childhood Development. National Academy Press.

   A comprehensive review of the science of early childhood development and its implications for policy and practice.

Websites and Online Resources

1. American Psychological Association. Parenting. Retrieved from [https://www.apa.org/topics/parenting]

   The APA provides a wealth of resources and research on parenting practices and child development.

2. Child Mind Institute. Resources for Parents. Retrieved from [https://childmind.org/]

   An organization offering support and resources for parents on various aspects of child mental health and development.

3. Edutopia. Social and Emotional Learning (SEL). Retrieved from [https://www.edutopia.org/sel]

   A resource for educators and parents on integrating social and emotional learning into education.

4. National Association for the Education of Young Children (NAEYC). For Families. Retrieved from [https://www.naeyc.org/families]

   NAEYC provides information and resources on early childhood education and development for families.

5. Zero to Three. Early Childhood Development. Retrieved from [https://www.zerotothree.org/]

   An organization dedicated to ensuring that all babies and toddlers have a strong start in life.

Addition Section:

Books and Articles

1. Dombro, A. L., Jablon, J. R., & Stetson, C. (2011). Powerful Interactions: How to Connect with Children to Extend Their Learning. National Association for the Education of Young Children.

2. Gartrell, D. (2007). Guidance Matters: Discipline in Early Childhood Education. Redleaf Press.

3. Gordon, A. M., & Browne, K. W. (2014). Beginnings & Beyond: Foundations in Early Childhood Education. Cengage Learning.

4. Kostelnik, M. J., Gregory, K., Soderman, A. K., & Whiren, A. P. (2015). Developmentally Appropriate Curriculum: Best Practices in Early Childhood Education. Pearson.

5. Roberts, C. A., & Crawford, P. A. (2008). Real Life Literacy: Classroom Tools that Promote Real-World Reading and Writing. International Reading Association.

6. Duffy, B. (2008). Supporting Creativity and Imagination in the Early Years. Open University Press.

Journals and Research Papers

1. National Association for the Education of Young Children (NAEYC). "Promoting Young Children's Social and Emotional Health." Retrieved from [NAEYC] (https://www.naeyc.org).

2. Centers for Disease Control and Prevention (CDC). "Learn About Child Development." Retrieved from [CDC](https://www.cdc.gov/ncbddd/childdevelopment/facts.html).

3. Harvard Graduate School of Education. "The Science of Early Childhood Development." Retrieved from [Harvard Graduate School of Education](https://www.gse.harvard.edu/news/uk/17/02/science-early-childhood-development).

Websites and Online Resources

1. American Psychological Association (APA). "Building Resilience in Children." Retrieved from [APA](https://www.apa.org/topics/resilience/children).

2. Child Mind Institute. "Mindfulness Practices for Children." Retrieved from [Child Mind Institute](https://childmind.org/article/mindfulness-exercises-for-kids/).

3. Understood.org. "Social and Emotional Learning: What You Need to Know." Retrieved from [Understood](https://www.understood.org/articles/en/social-emotional-learning-what-you-need-to-know).

———◆◆———

This bibliography reflects the extensive research and diverse sources that have informed the creation of "Emotional Edge in Parenting" I am deeply grateful to all the authors and researchers whose work has contributed to a deeper understanding of emotional development, parenting, and child education. Thank you for your invaluable contributions to this field.